T0002925

PROPOSALS TO ADDRESS
POLITICAL INTERFERENCE

Outcomes of a Trilateral Dialogue

EDITORS: SAMUEL CHARAP AND REINHARD KRUMM

Sponsored by Carnegie Corporation of New York

NATIONAL SECURITY RESEARCH DIVISION

For more information on this publication, visit **www.rand.org/t/CFA1775-1**.

About RAND

The RAND Corporation is a research organization that develops solutions to public policy challenges to help make communities throughout the world safer and more secure, healthier and more prosperous. RAND is nonprofit, nonpartisan, and committed to the public interest. To learn more about RAND, visit www.rand.org.

Research Integrity

Our mission to help improve policy and decisionmaking through research and analysis is enabled through our core values of quality and objectivity and our unwavering commitment to the highest level of integrity and ethical behavior. To help ensure our research and analysis are rigorous, objective, and nonpartisan, we subject our research publications to a robust and exacting quality-assurance process; avoid both the appearance and reality of financial and other conflicts of interest through staff training, project screening, and a policy of mandatory disclosure; and pursue transparency in our research engagements through our commitment to the open publication of our research findings and recommendations, disclosure of the source of funding of published research, and policies to ensure intellectual independence. For more information, visit www.rand.org/about/principles.

RAND's publications do not necessarily reflect the opinions of its research clients and sponsors.

Published by the RAND Corporation, Santa Monica, Calif.
© 2023 RAND Corporation
RAND® is a registered trademark.

Library of Congress Cataloging-in-Publication Data is available for this publication.
ISBN: 978-1-9774-1201-0

Limited Print and Electronic Distribution Rights

This publication and trademark(s) contained herein are protected by law. This representation of RAND intellectual property is provided for noncommercial use only. Unauthorized posting of this publication online is prohibited; linking directly to its webpage on rand.org is encouraged. Permission is required from RAND to reproduce, or reuse in another form, any of its research products for commercial purposes. For information on reprint and reuse permissions, please visit www.rand.org/pubs/permissions.

About This Paper

This document, finalized in January 2022 and not subsequently revised, explores the possibility of reaching agreements among the United States, Russia, and the European Union (EU) that relate to the issue of political interference. The paper sums up a series of discussions among U.S., Russian, and EU nongovernmental experts who were convened in 2020–2021 at the joint initiative of the RAND Corporation and the German nonprofit Friedrich Ebert Stiftung's Regional Office for Cooperation and Peace in Europe. These experts attempted to find common ground on potential measures to address the grievances of all sides concerning political interference. Geopolitical circumstances have changed dramatically since the proposals here were agreed on, and the current environment makes discussion of such matters at any level nearly impossible. Nonetheless, the proposals offer valuable input to potential future deliberations on such issues, if and when those deliberations become possible again.

RAND National Security Research Division

This project was sponsored by Carnegie Corporation of New York and conducted within the International Security and Defense Policy Center of the RAND National Security Research Division (NSRD).

For more information on the RAND International Security and Defense Policy Center, see www.rand.org/nsrd/isdp or contact the director (contact information is provided on the webpage).

Acknowledgments

We thank Carnegie Corporation of New York for its continuing support for this project in its current and earlier phases and the Friedrich Ebert Stiftung's Regional Office for Cooperation and Peace in Europe for its partnership. We are grateful to Jack Goldsmith and Elina Treyger for their thorough reviews and helpful comments on the draft. Additionally, we thank John Godges for his editorial wizardry and Melissa Shostak for her research assistance.

Foreword

The working group of Americans, Europeans, and Russians convened for this project finished its work in fall 2021, and this document was ready for publication in January 2022. In other words, this document was written before any of the events that have unfolded since February 2022 in Ukraine and, more broadly, in the relationship between Russia and the West. Since then, not only has the prospect of cooperation on nearly any issue, let alone a politically sensitive one such as this, become nearly inconceivable, but the facts on the ground in this domain—the legal environment and even the very nature of political systems—have also shifted dramatically. For example, our group recommended the consideration of mutual relaxation of regulations on foreign broadcasters (i.e., state-sponsored foreign-language media outlets, such as *Radio Free Europe/Radio Liberty*). Since February 2022, many of the relevant states' foreign broadcasters have been either sanctioned or essentially banned (or both) from the television and radio airwaves.

In this context, the proposals here might seem ill-timed at best. However, as the cyber expert Alexander Klimburg writes, "good policy needs to prepare for the day after tomorrow, and smart policy will look at what has gone wrong today and what can be learned from yesterday."[1] We, the conveners of this project, are confident that there is value in these proposals—particularly, given the consensus-building process we used to arrive at them—despite the reality that they are not viable under current circumstances. The issue of political interference has been overshadowed by other priorities, but it will inevitably return to the fore in Russia-West relations in the future. Having policy ideas on the shelf that can be considered when that time comes—particularly, ideas that were generated in a Track 2 process that included Americans, Russians, and Europeans—should be of value for all sides, even if the details of these proposals will have to be adapted to new realities.

---

[1] Alexander Klimburg, "Of Ships and Cyber: Transposing the Incidents at Sea Agreement," Center for Strategic and International Studies, September 28, 2022.

The participants in this project included nongovernmental experts in the areas of cybersecurity and international relations and in related issues. These experts came from the European Union, the United States, and Russia. They all approved this text, with the reservations noted in Appendix B. However, they did so before the events of February 2022; in the environment that now prevails, a collaborative project such as this would have been impossible. And some of them would likely not want to be associated with a publication such as this under current circumstances. In order to share the ideas generated by our project but avoid any possible challenges for the participants, we have decided to withhold their names.

We have preserved the text that the participants approved in January 2022 without any changes. Revising the document in 2023 would not only entail a fruitless attempt to stay ahead of rapidly shifting political winds, but it would also likely be impossible to reach agreement among the participants, underscoring the reality that the parties, even at the level of nongovernmental experts, cannot come to consensus about this or any other major topic. It should be underscored that no one is suggesting that September 2023 is the right time for governments to pursue these proposals. Indeed, as of this writing, it is difficult to imagine when the right time might come. But we remain hopeful that it will.

Contents

Tables

CHAPTER ONE

Introduction

This text was finalized in January 2022 and has not been subsequently revised.

In this paper, we explore the possibility of reaching agreements among the United States, Russia, and the European Union (EU) that relate to the issue of political interference. The paper sums up a series of discussions among U.S., Russian, and EU nongovernmental experts who were convened at the joint initiative of the RAND Corporation and the German foundation Friedrich Ebert Stiftung's Regional Office for Cooperation and Peace in Europe. Forced by the coronavirus disease 2019 (COVID-19) pandemic to meet virtually, we attempted through dialogue to achieve greater clarity on the grievances of all sides concerning political interference and to find common ground—the lowest common denominator, even—on potential measures to address those grievances.

The group's work was based on two assumptions. First, although the issue of foreign political interference in the digital age is a global one, mutual grievances regarding interference have had a particularly pernicious effect on relations between Russia and the West, injecting a dangerous level of instability in those relations and thus threatening international security by dramatically limiting the capacity of the parties to cooperatively address shared challenges. As we discuss in Chapter Two, Russia on the one hand and the EU and United States on the other harbor significant mutual grievances regarding interference. These grievances are central to mutual threat perceptions, which have become more acute in recent years. Concerns about interference were not the original causes of the downturn in relations and, in many ways, are functions of that downturn. But they have still had a dramatically negative impact. A core motivation behind this effort is that finding mutually acceptable ways to address interference could help to stabilize the relationship between Russia and the West. Doing so would also be consistent with the parties' obligations under the United Nations (UN) Charter to peacefully settle their disputes.[1] Of course, even if such efforts were successful, they would not fundamentally transform the relationship, which will remain competitive in some areas and adversarial in others. But more effective management of the interference issue could meaningfully contribute to stability.

Our second assumption was that the problem of interference cannot be effectively addressed without negotiated arrangements among affected governments. Such arrangements, which could range from coordinated (but not necessarily codified) actions to formal agreements, are only one necessary piece of the puzzle to effect a sustained improvement. Other, domestic policy measures not on our group's agenda—such as increased cyber defenses, greater societal resilience, and credible deterrent threats—are arguably just as important. But our group operated on the assumption that effective management of the interference problem would require not only such domestic steps but also international consultations and agreed-upon measures among the concerned states. We focused on what might be the content of those measures.

Current Russian and Western government policies on possible international agreements relating to this issue differ significantly. Russia has proposed a bilateral noninterference agreement with the United States since 2017 and has emphasized noninterference in its multilateral proposals relating to cybersecurity.[2] Western governments oppose these proposals, seeing them as attempts to regulate information in a way that undermines fundamental rights, such as freedom of expression, and generally seek to avoid any international agreement that could legitimize the regulation of con-

---

[1]   UN, Charter of the United Nations, San Francisco, June 26, 1945, Article 2, Section 3.

[2]   See, inter alia, Ministry of Foreign Affairs of the Russian Federation, "Brifing ofitsial'nogo predstavitelya MID Rossii M.V. Zakharovoi, Moskva, 28 dekabrya 2017 goda," webpage, December 28, 2017; UN Secretary-General, *Developments in the Field of Information and Telecommunications in the Context of International Security*, A/54/213, August 10, 1999, pp. 8–10; and U.S. Embassy in Russia, "Secretary Pompeo's Press Availability with Russian Foreign Minister Sergey Lavrov," May 14, 2019.

tent on the internet.[3] Their concern is that any new negotiations could call into question existing international law and norms, ultimately resulting in more uncertainty and more instability.[4] This paper should not be read as an explicit or implicit endorsement of either side of this debate; although we propose internationally agreed-upon measures relating to interference, our proposals differ considerably from those made by any government. We see the need for governments to address this issue in a manner that is mutually acceptable to them all; thus far, the approaches of all sides have not met this criterion. Our proposals could thread this needle. Although they would require flexibility from all parties, they could also provide significant benefits for all parties by mitigating the threat of foreign interference.

Scope and Process

The conveners brought together experts from the United States, the EU, and Russia to address a variety of issues that are relevant to the challenge of interference. The group included experts in cyber policy; specialists in the international normative issues relating to interference; computer security experts, including those with experience in the private sector; and specialists in relations between Russia and the West. The participants acted in their individual capacities, not as representatives of their respective employers or governments. The proposals in this document reflect our attempt to find consensus among the group members and are therefore unlikely to be consistent with any state's official positions.

The varied composition of the group reflected the cross-cutting nature of the subject at hand. Interference overlaps with some, but not all, of the issues

---

[3]   See, for example, U.S. Department of State, *Department of State International Cyberspace Policy Strategy*, March 2016.

[4]   In October 2021, the United States and Russia were the coauthors of a UN General Assembly resolution on related issues, indicating at least a partial rapprochement. However, the resolution mostly concerns process and does not suggest a fundamental convergence on long-standing disputes (UN General Assembly, "Developments in the Field of Information and Telecommunications in the Context of International Security, and Advancing Responsible State Behaviour in the Use of Information and Communications Technologies," October 8, 2021).

traditionally under the rubric of cybersecurity. Put differently, the parties' concerns relating to cyberspace go far beyond interference, and, conversely, interference is not just a "cyber" issue. Therefore, we did not discuss several traditional cyber issues that do not relate to interference. For example, we did not address computer network exploitation conducted exclusively for intelligence-gathering purposes; cyberattacks on critical infrastructure, except for those elements (such as election infrastructure) that are directly relevant to political processes; ransomware; economic espionage; etc. Furthermore, because alleged political interference is not exclusive to cyberspace, we did not limit ourselves to the cyber domain. We considered noncyber issues, such as state-funded foreign-language broadcasters, in addition to interference in the cyber domain.

The EU, U.S., and Russian groups first met separately to discuss these issues. Subsequently, all participants met in four sessions conducted over Zoom. Additional side meetings were conducted among smaller subgroups to work out the details of our proposals. The specific issues discussed included the challenge of developing a shared definition of interference and noninterference, the nature of the parties' respective grievances, state-sponsored activities on social media, possible cyberattacks on election infrastructure, hack-and-leak operations, confidence-building measures related to interference, and the appropriate regulation of state-owned media or, more specifically, foreign-language broadcasters.

Although we focus on areas where we could find common ground, our discussions highlighted several important divergences among European, U.S., and Russian approaches to these issues. All sides have major concerns about foreign interference, but their specific grievances do not overlap completely. We elaborate on those differences in Chapter Two.

The recommendations here do not fit neatly into a particular multilateral process or bilateral negotiating format, which reflects the fact that interference does not have its own diplomatic "lane." Instead, interference-related issues are handled in multiple contexts. We are not suggesting that interference should be given its own lane. Governments are in a better position to decide which formats and processes would be most appropriate. Our discussions focused on the substance of potential measures, not the choice of diplomatic processes.

A similar caveat applies to the form in which these proposals could be implemented. We do not address whether these measures should be implemented through politically binding or legally binding documents or whether coordinated but not formalized steps would be preferable to formal documents. The governments have divergent views on this issue, and we do not offer a recommendation. Although we focused on the substance of the possible measures, we recognize that crafting a diplomatic strategy for negotiating them might pose an equally daunting challenge.

Because we did not account for form or format when devising our proposals, they are not exclusively intergovernmental; rather, some would require changes to be implemented in national legislation or regulations. Because the core issues addressed by the proposals have become matters of international dispute, governments could coordinate changes made at the national level through an intergovernmental negotiation to help defuse interstate tensions.

It is important to note that interference-related issues cut across the respective competencies of EU member-state governments and of EU institutions. As a result, EU institutions likely do not have the authority to negotiate on behalf of the member states on all the issues covered by our proposals. However, the leadership of EU institutions could be empowered to lead consultations on interference, if the member states so choose.

Although we approached the interference issue in the context of the relationship between Russia and the West because of the corrosive impact it has had on that relationship, the issue affects a far larger number of states than Russia, the United States, and the EU member states. Therefore, a "first-track" trilateral negotiation of these issues might not be the best forum to address them; there is a case for doing so instead via broader processes, such as those based at the UN, or in a series of bilateral formats, such as between the United States and Russia, the EU and Russia, and beyond. However, interference remains a central issue in relations between Russia and the West, and therefore some form of trilateral consultations could be a useful mechanism to begin to address the issue. Certainly, our proposals were enriched by having all three perspectives represented in the discussions.

Although the proposals that we recommend in Chapter Three are directed toward governments, many of the actors involved in interference are nonstate actors, including commercial entities, proxy groups, nongovernmental organizations (NGOs), and private citizens. Therefore, some of these proposals would require states to act within their domestic jurisdictions to regulate relevant nonstate actors. Such a dynamic is not unique to this sphere; for instance, the Paris Climate Agreement will be implemented through the domestic regulation of private actors.

Finally, we considered only mutual interference: allegations of Russian interference in the West and of Western interference in Russia. The activities of these parties in other countries were beyond the scope of our discussions.

CHAPTER TWO

Grievances Related to Political Interference

This text was finalized in January 2022 and has not been subsequently revised.

Although Russia and the West both voice concerns about interference, the specific activities they view as problematic differ significantly.[1] In this section, we describe the official U.S. and EU allegations of Russian interference in the United States and the EU, respectively, and the official Russian allegations of Western interference in Russia. As much as possible, we rely on official statements and government documents, rather than nongovernmental expert analysis or press reporting. We focus only on allegations of mutual interference, not on allegations of Russian or Western interference in other countries nor on those countries' interference activities.

The three groups drafted these sections separately. They therefore do not represent the shared or mutually agreed-on views of all participants. Further, it should be noted that essentially all the allegations described here have been officially denied by the party accused. None of the governments have ever admitted to engaging in acts of prohibited interference.

---

[1]   We focus exclusively on grievances in the interference domain, although clearly this domain is far from the only one in which Russia and the West have significant mutual grievances.

U.S. Grievances

The U.S. government has alleged that Russia and Russian-backed actors have interfered in U.S. politics and elections since 2014.[2] These allegations include assertions that Russian actors have engaged in the following forms of political interference: hack-and-leak operations, cyber threats to U.S. election infrastructure, state-sponsored influence campaigns on social media, and the publication of propaganda and socially manipulative content on Russian government–sponsored English-language media. Concerns about these activities have been reported by numerous U.S. government agencies.

Much of the focus has been on alleged Russian government and government-sponsored actions during the 2016 presidential election. Activities that the U.S. government has alleged that the Russian government undertook or sponsored during this election cycle include the hack-and-leak campaign against the Clinton campaign, cyber intrusions into state election infrastructure, social media campaigns to sow social discord in the United States, and the publication of manipulative news on Russian government–affiliated news sites, such as Sputnik.[3] However, the U.S. government has also alleged Russian interference in both the 2018 midterm elections and the 2020 presidential elections, indicating that the United States sees Russian intrusion into U.S. politics and elections as an ongoing threat.[4]

---

[2] Office of the Special Counsel, *Report on the Investigation into Russian Interference in the 2016 Presidential Election*, Vol. 1, Washington, D.C.: U.S. Department of Justice, March 2019, p. 14.

[3] Heather H. Hunt, Chief of the FARA Registration Unit, Department of Justice, "Obligation of RIA Global LLC to Register Under the Foreign Agents Registration Act," letter to Mindia Gavasheli, Peter Martinichev, and Anastasia Sheveleva at RIA Global LLC, Washington, D.C., January 5, 2018, p. 5; United States v. Internet Research Agency et al., No. 1:18-cr-32, D.D.C. February 16, 2018, Doc. 1 ("Internet Research Agency Indictment"), pp. 3–4; United States v. Netyksho et al., No. 1: 18-cr-15, D.D.C. July 13, 2018, Doc. 1 ("Netyksho Indictment"), pp. 1–3; and U.S. Senate Select Committee on Intelligence, *Russian Active Measures Campaigns and Interference in the 2016 U.S. Election*, Vol. 1: *Russian Efforts Against Election Infrastructure*, 116th Congress, 1st Session, Senate Report 116-XX, undated a, p. 12.

[4] National Intelligence Council, *Foreign Threats to the 2020 US Federal Elections*, Washington, D.C., ICA 2020-00078D, March 10, 2021, pp. 2–3.

Hack-and-Leak Operations

The U.S. government alleges that Russian military intelligence hacked into the networks of the Democratic Congressional Campaign Committee, the Democratic National Committee, and the presidential campaign of Hillary Clinton in the spring of 2016. Documents from these hacks were then leaked to WikiLeaks and the press through the fabricated "DCLeaks" and "Guccifer 2.0" personas.[5] The 2019 Mueller Report alleges that these documents were leaked at key points in the presidential campaign to undermine U.S. confidence in both the election system and Hillary Clinton.[6]

Cyber Threats to U.S. Election Infrastructure

U.S. government documents and statements from officials allege that the Russian government gained access to some U.S. election infrastructure, including voter registration databases, during the 2016, 2018, and 2020 elections. These reports emphasize that Russian access to U.S. election infrastructure did not affect the vote tallies or the outcomes of the elections.[7]

For example, former Special Assistant to the President and Cybersecurity Coordinator Michael Daniel testified to the Senate Intelligence Committee that, by the end of the 2016 election cycle, Russian government actors had attempted to gain access to election infrastructure in all 50 U.S. states.[8] Reports from the U.S. intelligence community and the Department of Homeland Security state that these efforts were oriented around gathering intelligence on the U.S. election system rather than actively manipulating election infrastructure.[9] Similar efforts in 2018 and 2020 to gain access

---

[5] Office of the Special Counsel, 2019, pp. 36–48.

[6] Office of the Special Counsel, 2019, p. 36.

[7] Jeremy Herb, Brian Fung, Jennifer Hansler, and Zachary Cohen, "Russian Hackers Targeting State and Local Governments Have Stolen Data, US Officials Say," *CNN,* October 23, 2020; and U.S. Senate Select Committee on Intelligence, undated a, pp. 3, 10–11, 22.

[8] U.S. Senate Select Committee on Intelligence, undated a, p. 12.

[9] U.S. Senate Select Committee on Intelligence, undated a, pp. 10–11.

to U.S. election infrastructure reportedly were again focused on gathering intelligence rather than manipulating the election results.[10]

State-Sponsored Influence Campaigns

The U.S. government has claimed that Russian government entities and state-sponsored actors have executed influence campaigns aimed at "interfering with the U.S. political and electoral processes."[11] Reports from the U.S. intelligence community assert that Russian efforts to craft influence campaigns date back to at least 2014.[12] Evidence of Russian state-sponsored influence campaigns was recorded during the 2016 presidential elections, 2018 midterms, and 2020 presidential elections.[13]

The most significant examples concerned "Project Lakhta," which allegedly attempted to undermine the U.S. political system through the systematic distribution of misinformation and disinformation on social media.[14] Efforts associated with Project Lakhta included running the Internet Research Agency "troll farm" to spread disinformation during the 2016 presidential elections and the 2018 midterm elections.[15]

---

[10] Herb et al., 2020; U.S. Senate Select Committee on Intelligence, undated a, p. 22.

[11] United States of America v. Internet Research Agency, 2018, pp. 2–3.

[12] United States of America v. Internet Research Agency, 2018, p. 3.

[13] Director of National Intelligence, "DNI Coats Statement on the Intelligence Community's Response to Executive Order 13848 on Imposing Certain Sanctions in the Event of Foreign Interference in a United States Election," press release, Washington, D.C., December 21, 2018; National Intelligence Council, 2021, p. 2; and U.S. Senate Select Committee on Intelligence, *Russian Active Measures Campaigns and Interference in the 2016 U.S. Election*, Vol. 2: *Russia's Use of Social Media*, 116th Congress, 1st Session, Senate Report 116-XX, undated b, p. 5.

[14] U.S. Department of Justice, "Russian National Charged with Interfering in U.S. Political System," press release, Washington, D.C., October 19, 2018.

[15] Cory Welt, Kristin Archick, Rebecca M. Nelson, and Dianne E. Rennack, *U.S. Sanctions on Russia*, Washington, D.C.: Congressional Research Service, R45415, January 17, 2020, pp. 17–18.

Publication of Propaganda and Socially Manipulative Content on Foreign Government–Sponsored English-Language Media

The U.S. government has also alleged that Russian government–sponsored English-language media has published pro-Russian propaganda and content intended to manipulate U.S. audiences and decrease trust in the U.S. government. Russian media outlets tied to these allegations include RT (formerly *Russia Today*) and *Sputnik*, which were forced to register under the 1938 Foreign Agents Registration Act (FARA) because of their perceived promotion of pro-Kremlin propaganda.[16] As former Federal Bureau of Investigation (FBI) Director James Comey claimed, "The Kremlin is waging an international disinformation campaign through the RT propaganda network which traffics in anti-American conspiracy theories that rivaled the extravagant untruths of Soviet era Pravda."[17]

The U.S. claims that Russian government–sponsored media have also spread disinformation regarding the COVID-19 pandemic. This includes spreading rumors that COVID-19 is a hacked U.S. biological weapon rather than a naturally occurring virus and disinformation regarding the safety and efficacy of Western COVID-19 vaccines.[18] Disinformation on COVID-19 has also been published on sites that the U.S. Department of State claims are Kremlin-linked proxy sites for propaganda and disinformation.[19]

---

[16] Heather H. Hunt, Chief of the FARA Registration Unit, Department of Justice, "Obligation of RTTV America, Inc., to Register Under the Foreign Agents Registration Act," letter to RTTV America, Inc., Washington, D.C., August 17, 2017; and Hunt, 2018.

[17] "Full transcript: FBI Director James Comey Testifies on Russian Interference in 2016 Election," *Washington Post*, March 20, 2017.

[18] Deirdre Shesgreen, "'Russia Is Up to Its Old Tricks': Biden Battling COVID-19 Vaccine Disinformation Campaign," *USA Today*, March 8, 2021; and Catherine A. Theohary, "Considering the Source: Varieties of COVID-19 Information," Washington, D.C.: Congressional Research Service, IF11552, May 19, 2020.

[19] U.S. Department of State, Global Engagement Center, *Pillars of Russia's Disinformation and Propaganda Ecosystem*, Washington, D.C., August 2020, pp. 12–13, 31–33, 37–45.

European Union Grievances

The EU and its member states have voiced a variety of concerns regarding Russian interference in the functioning of their societies and democratic processes and institutions. Most of these concerns fall under the broad umbrella of hybrid warfare.[20] Russian efforts, used to target not only the EU but also its strategic partners and allies,[21] have allegedly included three types of Russian political interference: disinformation and other forms of information manipulation, the financing of political parties and other extreme groups, and hack-and-leak operations.

Disinformation and Other Forms of Information Manipulation

At the EU level, concerns about foreign interference, particularly from Russia, have been raised repeatedly.[22] In 2015, the European Council called for an action plan on strategic communication "to challenge Russia's ongoing disinformation campaigns."[23] The EU's concerns about disinformation relate both to propaganda and socially manipulative content put forth by foreign government–sponsored traditional media broadcasting in local languages and to often-related influence campaigns on social media.

---

[20] European Commission, *Joint Framework on Countering Hybrid Threats: A European Union Response*, Brussels, JOIN(2016)18, April 6, 2016.

[21] Although the focus of this section is on interference only on the EU territory, the EU's grievances cannot be detached from the EU's broader concerns regarding Russia's disrespect for international law, violations of human rights, and shrinking space for the opposition, civil society, and independent voices across Russia (European Council, "Russia: Declaration by the High Representative on Behalf of the European Union on the State Duma, Regional and Local Elections," press release, Brussels, September 20, 2021).

[22] See, generally, European Parliament, "EU to Take Action Against Fake News and Foreign Election Interference," press release, Brussels, October 10, 2019.

[23] European Council, "European Council Meeting (19 and 20 March 2015) – Conclusions," Brussels, EUCO 11/15, March 20, 2015.

In a 2018 communication on tackling online disinformation,[24] the EU expressed concern over growing obstacles to obtaining the objective information that serves as the basis for constructive public debate and informed decisionmaking.[25] In particular, the EU concluded that disinformation (1) erodes trust in institutions and in digital and traditional media, (2) harms democracies by hampering the ability of citizens to make informed decisions, (3) often supports radical and extremist ideas and activities, and (4) impairs freedom of expression, a fundamental right enshrined in the Charter of Fundamental Rights of the EU.[26]

Foreign actors sowing distrust and creating societal tensions through online disinformation campaigns are seen as having serious potential consequences for EU security. Russia is often linked to disinformation campaigns that are part of hybrid warfare. A 2019 report on the EU's Action Plan Against Disinformation noted *"continued and sustained"* disinformation activity from Russian sources—activity that the EU regards as "aiming to suppress turnout and influence voter preferences."[27] Disinformation from Russian sources about COVID-19 has also been singled out in EU policy on disinformation.[28] The EU is also concerned about Russia's reliance on

---

[24] European Commission, Directorate-General for Communications Networks, Content and Technology, *Tackling Online Disinformation: A European Approach*, COM(2018)236 final, April 26, 2018.

[25] European Commission, Directorate-General for Communications Networks, Content and Technology, 2018, pp. 1–2.

[26] European Commission, Directorate-General for Communications Networks, Content and Technology, 2018, pp. 1–2.

[27] European Commission, *Report on the Implementation of the Action Plan Against Disinformation*, Brussels, JOIN(2019)12, June 14, 2019.

[28] See, for instance, European Commission, Directorate-General for Justice and Consumers, *Commission Recommendation on Election Cooperation Networks, Online Transparency, Protection Against Cybersecurity Incidents and Fighting Disinformation Campaigns in the Context of Elections to the European Parliament: A Contribution from the European Commission to the Leaders' Meeting in Salzburg on 19-20 September 2018*, Brussels, C(2018)5949, September 12, 2018a; European Commission, Directorate-General for Justice and Consumers, *Securing Free and Fair European Elections: A Contribution from the European Commission to the Leaders' Meeting in Salzburg on 19-20 September 2018*, Brussels, COM(2018)637, September 12, 2018b; European Commission, Directorate-General for Justice and Consumers, *Commission Guidance on the Applica-*

manipulative tactics to undermine democratic debate and exacerbate social polarization.

The gravity of these concerns has been expressed through concrete EU legislative and institutional adaptations, including the creation of the East StratCom Task Force in the European External Action Service and the establishment of a network of fact checkers known as the European Digital Media Observatory. To date, the East StratCom Task Force has cataloged, analyzed, and put the spotlight on over 4,500 examples of disinformation by the Russian Federation, including campaigns that undermine the EU's global position and values in the context of the Syrian civil war, the downing of flight MH17 in eastern Ukraine in 2014, and the use of chemical weapons in the 2018 Salisbury attack.

Financing of Political Parties and Other Extreme Groups

The funding of European political parties is governed by EU and member-state law. Over the past several years, there have been various allegations of Russia providing funding for separatist forces, antiestablishment parties, and other groups on the extreme fringes of the political spectrum within the EU "with the intent of undermining political cohesion."[29] For instance, the French Front National obtained a €9.4-million loan from a Russian bank in September 2014.[30]

---

tion of Union Data Protection Law in the Electoral Context: A Contribution from the European Commission to the Leaders' Meeting in Salzburg on 19-20 September 2018, Brussels, COM(2018)638, October 1, 2018c; and European Parliament and Council of the European Union, Regulation (EU, Euratom) 2019/493 of the European Parliament and of the Council of 25 March 2019 Amending Regulation (EU, Euratom) No 1141/2014 as Regards a Verification Procedure Related to Infringements of Rules on the Protection of Personal Data in the Context of Elections to the European Parliament, March 27, 2019, pp. 7–10. See also European Commission, High Representative of the Union for Foreign Affairs and Security Policy, *Tackling COVID-19 Disinformation – Getting the Facts Right,* Brussels, JOIN(2020)8, June 10, 2020.

[29] European Parliament, Resolution of 23 November 2016 on EU Strategic Communication to Counteract Propaganda Against It by Third Parties, TA(2016)0441, November 23, 2016.

[30] Gabriel Gatehouse, "Marine Le Pen: Who's Funding France's Far Right?" *BBC News,* April 3, 2017.

In other cases, such direct evidence might be missing, but many European officials are convinced that Russia is covertly supporting radical groups across Europe. In 2017, the European People's Party—the largest party grouping in the European Parliament—published a position paper on Russia, deploring

> Russia's attempts to undermine democratic processes in European societies, including through the systematic and strategic use of disinformation and propaganda, as well as through support for and the financing of radical and extremist parties both inside and outside the EU.[31]

Hack-and-Leak Operations

There have been a variety of allegations of Russian state agencies hacking European politicians and political institutions and then leaking the information for political effect. The most prominent example was the so-called Macron Leaks, in which a large cache of hacked data from French President Emmanuel Macron and his campaign was made public on the eve of the second round of the French presidential elections in 2017.[32] Although the French government has not formally attributed the attack to Russian state actors, the U.S. Department of Justice provided fairly detailed evidence in a 2020 indictment.[33]

The United Kingdom (UK) government has alleged that Russian operatives hacked and then leaked sensitive documents related to U.S.-UK trade talks during the 2019 general election campaign. "On the basis of extensive analysis, the government has concluded that it is almost certain that Russian actors sought to interfere in the 2019 general election through the online

---

[31] European People's Party, "Position Paper on Russia," Brussels, September 27, 2017.

[32] Jean-Baptiste Jeangène Vilmer, "Lessons of #MacronLeaks," *Berlin Policy Journal*, August 29, 2019.

[33] U.S. Department of Justice, "Six Russian GRU Officers Charged in Connection with Worldwide Deployment of Destructive Malware and Other Disruptive Actions in Cyberspace," press release, Washington, D.C., October 19, 2020.

amplification of illicitly acquired and leaked government documents," said then–UK Foreign Secretary Dominic Raab.[34]

In Germany, there have been widespread reports of Russian state–led hacks of the Bundestag, politicians, and political parties. Ahead of the German parliamentary elections in September 2021, German federal prosecutors confirmed that they were probing alleged hacking attacks against lawmakers and that they believed the attacks came from Russia. Germany accused Russia of using phishing attacks to gain access to the personal log-in data of members of Parliament—data that ultimately could serve as "preparation for an influence operation, for example a disinformation campaign, in the general election."[35] However, as of this writing, none of this hacked information has been made public.

Russian Grievances

Senior Russian officials have raised concerns about foreign political interference for years. According to Russia's 2021 National Security Strategy, prevention of interference in the internal affairs of the Russian state is of vital importance; it is listed as the first task for ensuring the security of the state and the polity as a whole. That document goes on to state that "the use of information-communication technologies for interference in the internal affairs of states . . . poses a threat to international peace and security."[36]

Russia has a broad range of grievances when it comes to interference. In some cases, the grievances are described in general terms.[37] In other

---

[34] Dan Sabbagh, "UK Says Russia Sought to Interfere in 2019 Election by Spreading Documents Online," *The Guardian*, July 16, 2020.

[35] Agence France-Presse, "Germany Probes Claims of Pre-Election MP Hacking by Russia," *France24*, September 9, 2021; and Loveday Morris, "Germany Complains to Moscow over Pre-Election Phishing Attacks on Politicians," *Washington Post*, September 6, 2021.

[36] President of Russia, "Prezident utverdil Strategiyu natsional'noi bezopasnosti," July 2, 2021.

[37] For example, in his 2020 interview speaking in the context of interference, Secretary of the Security Council Nikolai Patrushev described how foreign NGOs use Russian NGOs that participate in political activities and mentioned funding that Russian NGOs

instances, to paint a broad picture, Russian officials name multiple specific situations that they consider to be cases of foreign interference. This approach is best illustrated in the work of the Federation Council's Interim Commission on Protecting State Sovereignty and Preventing Interference in the Domestic Affairs of the Russian Federation, particularly in its annual reports.[38] (The Federation Council is the upper house of the Russian parliament. The lower house has a similar entity, called the Duma Commission for Investigating Interference by Foreign States in Russia's Domestic Affairs; however, its activity is less noticeable.)

The Federation Council's Interim Commission first convened in 2017, prior to the Russian presidential elections in 2018. Its primary task was to conduct hearings and gather and analyze evidence about foreign interference. The commission published three annual reports: in 2018 (prior to the presidential elections), 2019, and 2020 (prior to the vote on amendments to the constitution). The first report is of special interest because it provides the very first comprehensive articulation of Russia's official definition of *foreign interference*:

> the activity of foreign governments, organizations, or individuals aimed at changing Russia's constitutional order, territorial integrity, domestic and foreign policies, or the structure and composition of governmental and municipal bodies, in contravention of international law and Russia's international agreements.[39]

According to official statements and policies, Russia's grievances regarding foreign interference can be categorized as follows: foreign funding of political activities, foreign government–sponsored media, politically

---

received from abroad (Vitalii Tseplyaev, "Kuklovodstvo k deistviyu. Nikolai Patrushev – o metodakh 'tsvetnykh revolyutsii'," *Argumenty i fakty*, June 10, 2020).

[38] Federation Council, "Vremennaya kommissiya Soveta Federatsii po zashchite gosudarstvennogo suvereniteta i predotvarashcheniyu vmeshatel'stva vo vnutrennie dela Rossiiskoi Federatsii," webpage, undated.

[39] Federation Council, *Ezhegodnyi doklad Vremennoi komissii Soveta Federatsii po zashchite gosudarstvennogo suvereniteta i predotvarashcheniyu vmeshatel'stva vo vnutrennie dela Rossiiskoi Federatsii*, Moscow, June 15, 2020a.

motivated leaks or forgeries, cyber threats to elections, and other types of interference.

Foreign Funding of Political Activities

One of the major concerns for Russia is alleged foreign funding of individuals and organizations involved in politics. Russia's understanding of what constitutes political activity is broad and includes not only explicitly political entities, such as parties or politicians, but also nongovernmental and other types of organizations whose work might be connected to political issues.

The prominence of foreign-funded NGOs among Russia's concerns can be traced back to the mid-2000s and the role of the nongovernmental sector, as perceived by some Russian officials and commentators, in the popular uprisings known as "color revolutions" in neighboring states. Starting in 2005, the government more actively sought to tighten control of NGOs.[40] In 2012, the law on NGOs was amended to allow labeling them as foreign agents if they received money from abroad and were involved in political activities. The definition of what constitutes "political activity" has broadened, as indicated by the steady growth in the number of NGOs on the foreign-agent register over the past decade. Applying the foreign agent label to, for example, a civic organization working on domestic violence implies that ostensibly nonpolitical NGOs are assumed to be involved in political activities under the guise of their seemingly benign missions.[41]

Russia has worked to curtail foreign (primarily U.S.) funding for NGOs. In 2012, Russia expelled the U.S. Agency for International Development on the grounds that its activities included "attempts to influence the political process through the distribution of grants, including elections of different levels, and civil institutions,"[42] of which Russia said it warned the Ameri-

---

[40] Dmitrii Kamyshev, Mikhail Zygar', Irina Nagornykh, and Viktor Khamraev, "Vladimir Putin ostavil za soboi finansirovanie obshchestvennosti," *Kommersant*, November 25, 2005, p. 1.

[41] "Tsentr 'Nasiliyu.net' priznali inostrannym agentom," *Novaya gazeta*, December 29, 2020.

[42] Ministry of Foreign Affairs of the Russian Federation, "Comments of A.K. Lukashevicha, Official Representative of the Ministry of Foreign Affairs of Russia on the

cans many times. In 2015, the government adopted legislation on undesirable organizations through which it could declare a foreign or international NGO undesirable on the grounds that its activities posed a threat to the foundations of the constitutional order, national defense, or the security of the state. Two months after the law was adopted, the first organization to be declared undesirable was the National Endowment for Democracy, a grant-making body funded by the U.S. Congress that continues to sponsor projects in Russia. (However, unlike in other countries, the National Endowment for Democracy does not publicly identify Russian grantees by name.) In the ensuing months and years, Russia labeled other organizations as undesirable, including the International Republican Institute, the Black Sea Trust for Regional Cooperation, the European Endowment for Democracy, think tanks (such as the Atlantic Council), and private foundations.

By the late 2010s, such designations sharply curtailed foreign-funded NGO activities in Russia, as acknowledged in the 2018 Special Report of the Federation Council's Interim Commission.[43] Yet Russian officials continue to identify foreign funding as a serious concern. In the same report, the commission suggested that "shady schemes" are used to elude Russia's legal restrictions by, for example, providing financial support in the form of cash or wiring money to individuals. In July 2021, the Duma Commission for Investigating Interference by Foreign States in Russia's Domestic Affairs said that election webinars for Russians, which were organized by the National Democratic Institute (designated an undesirable organization in Russia), constituted training of influence agents. Consequently, the Duma Commission called for access to the National Democratic Institute's online resources to be blocked.[44]

Termination of Activities of the United States Agency of International Development of the Russian Federation," webpage, September 19, 2012.

[43] Vremennaya komissiya Soveta Federatsii po zashchite gosudarstvennogo suvereniteta i pretvarashcheniyu vmeshatel'stva vo vnutrennie dela Rossiiskoi Federatsii, *Spetsial'nyi doklad po itogam prezidentskikh vyborov v Rossiiskoi Federatsii (2018 g.) s tochki zreniya pokushenii na rossiiskoi elektoral'nyi suverenitet*, Moscow: Sovet Federatsii, undated, p. 7.

[44] State Duma of the Federal Assembly of the Russian Federation, "Komissiya GD vyyavila novye popytki povliyat' na khod izbiranel'noi kampanii v Rossii," webpage, July 15, 2021.

Foreign Government–Sponsored Media

As reflected in the reports of the Federation Council's Interim Commission, Russian authorities consider Western government–sponsored media to be tools of propaganda.[45] The Russian government has accused Western government–funded outlets of fomenting unrest and supporting opposition politicians. The Western outlets that have been particularly singled out are Radio Free Europe/Radio Liberty (RFE/RL), Voice of America (VOA), Deutsche Welle (DW), and the British Broadcasting Company (BBC).

These outlets are believed to be guided by Western political priorities and believed to be used to apply external pressure on Russia and to interfere in its domestic affairs. Coverage critical of Russia is often referred to as "informational support" for the opposition in Russia or seen as a mechanism aimed at destabilizing the Russian domestic situation and provoking antigovernment protests. As of 2017, the Russian government can brand media outlets as foreign agents. In December 2017, the first nine media outlets to be put on this list all were parts of the RFE/RL network, followed by two more RFE/RL outlets and a Czech media outlet in 2019 and 2020. In 2021, the government broadened the scope of this legal instrument and declared several organizations that were founded and staffed primarily by Russian nationals to be foreign agents on the grounds that they received foreign funding.[46]

Politically Motivated Leaks or Forgeries

On several occasions, Russian officials alleged that leaks containing politically sensitive information were perpetrated or supported by the West and constituted attempts to interfere in Russia's domestic affairs and discredit its leadership.

---

[45] See Vremennaya komissiya Soveta Federatsii po zashchite gosudarstvennogo suvereniteta i pretvarashcheniyu vmeshatel'stva vo vnutrennie dela Rossiiskoi Federatsii, undated, p. 22.

[46] Ministry of Justice of the Russian Federation, "Reestr inostrannykh sredstv massovo informatsii, vypolyayushchikh funktsii nostrannogo agenta," webpage, September 3, 2021.

The 2016 Panama Papers leak about the offshore finance industry is a case in point. The Kremlin argued that the main target of the leak was Russian President Vladimir Putin, with the intent of undermining political stability in Russia.[47] Putin also suggested that U.S. officials and agencies were behind the "assignment" to frame the story in this way.[48]

In 2019, an unnamed source told the wire service RIA Novosti that U.S. and British intelligence agencies were preparing disinformation on Putin's circle and on the leadership of the Ministry of Defense to justify additional sanctions. According to the source, the campaign would repeat the Panama Papers scenario, in which information beneficial to the West would be leaked to the media via NGOs affiliated with the U.S. Department of State.[49]

Cyber Threats to Elections

The Russian Central Elections Commission (CEC) has reported repeated attacks against its website during key elections. Although officials do not attribute such attacks to particular actors, they usually say the attacks come from abroad or use foreign infrastructure.

For instance, during the 2012 presidential election, the CEC said that its website was "subjected to massive attacks by hackers [including ones from] Western Europe and Australia."[50] In March 2018, during the most recent presidential election, the CEC reported that it suffered a distributed denial-of-service (DDoS) attack that used internet protocol (IP) addresses from 15 countries.[51] Russian law enforcement also reported that the computerized system used to tally votes was attacked in 2018.[52] During the 2020 vote on

---

[47] "Peskov: Putin ne figuriruet v publikatsii o tainykh ofshornykh schetakh," *RIA Novosti*, April 4, 2016.

[48] President of Russia, "Truth and Justice Regional and Local Media Forum," April 7, 2016.

[49] "SShA i Britaniya gotovyat feiki ob okruzhenii Putina, soobshchil istochnik," *RIA Novosti*, July 13, 2019.

[50] "Khakery usilenno atakuyut sait TsIK Rossii," *RIA Novosti*, March 4, 2012.

[51] "V den' vyborov otrazhena DDoS-ataka na sait TsIK s IP-adresov 15 stran," *TASS*, March 18, 2018.

[52] "MVD soobshchilo o kiberatake na GAS 'Vybory,'" *Kommersant*, March 18, 2018.

constitutional amendments, DDoS attacks targeted the CEC and other government bodies; according to the IP addresses, the sources of these attacks included the United States and the UK.[53] In the run-up to the 2021 Duma Elections, the head of the CEC said that most attacks on its website also originated from the United States and the UK.[54]

Social Media Manipulation

The Russian leadership has long been concerned about the possibility that internet-enabled communication generally, and social media in particular, could be used as a means of foreign interference. As Putin wrote in a 2012 article,

> The Internet, social media, mobile telephones, and so on have become an effective instrument of both domestic and foreign policy . . . Often they are used for cultivating and provoking extremism, separatism, nationalism, manipulation of public consciousness, and direct interference in internal affairs of sovereign states.[55]

Recently, actions demonstrating alleged bias by U.S.-based social media and other internet platforms against the Russian government and flouting Russian election law are also viewed as cases of interference. Russia's National Security Strategy condemns the platforms' "censorship" and distorted portrayal of Russia and its history.[56] The Interim Commission cites a case in which YouTube reportedly allowed political commercials during the day of silence before the 2018 elections.[57] In another example, Russia's Federal

---

[53] "Pri golosovanii po konstitutsii v RF fiksirovali DDoS-ataki iz SShA, Velikobritanii, Ukrainy," *TASS*, September 7, 2020.

[54] "TsIK RF soobshchil o regulyarnykh kiberatakakh na svoi sait iz SShA i Velikobritanii," *Interfax*, June 22, 2021.

[55] Vladimir Putin, "Rossiya i menyayushchiisya mir," *Moskovskie novosti*, February 27, 2012.

[56] President of Russia, 2021.

[57] Vremennaya komissiya Soveta Federatsii po zashchite gosudarstvennogo suvereniteta i predotvarashcheniyu vmeshatel'stva vo vnutrennie dela Rossiiskoi Federatsii, *Ezhegodnyi doklad*, Moscow: Sovet Federatsii, May 30, 2019.

Service for Supervision of Communications, Information Technology and Mass Media in 2019 accused Facebook and Google of not complying with the day of silence and said such actions could be regarded as interference in Russia's sovereign affairs.[58]

Other Types of Interference

Russian officials denounce other types of activities as foreign political interference. For instance, the Kremlin, the Federation Council's Interim Commission, and other senior officials have referred to sanctions on Russia as a form of interference.[59] Some actions of Western diplomats in Russia have been characterized by the authorities as interference in domestic affairs, generally having to do with alleged support for political opposition or protests.[60] The Interim Commission has condemned Western government funding of polling groups and focus groups in Russia, citing one example of a U.S. Department of Defense grant being used for this purpose.

Western governments' public statements about Russia's elections are also viewed as acts of interference. Putin and other senior officials specifically mentioned then–Secretary of State Hillary Clinton's criticism of the 2011

---

[58] Georgii Tadtaev and Anna Balashova, "Roskomadzor obvinil Facebook i Google vo vmeshatel'stve v vybory v Rossii," *RBC*, September 8, 2019. See also "Roskomnadzor schel vmeshatel'stvom v vybory blokirovku instagrama Prilepina," *Interfax*, July 23, 2021.

[59] Kira Latukhina, "Peskov nazval novye sanktsii SShA i ES vmeshatel'stvom v dela Rossii," *Rossiiskaya Gazeta*, March 3, 2021.

[60] In summer 2019, amid the backdrop of the Moscow City Duma electoral campaign, the Ministry of Foreign Affairs (MFA) decried the warning about upcoming protests published online by the U.S. Embassy and U.S. Department of State's Bureau of Consular Affairs. The MFA summoned the U.S. Deputy Chief of Mission and communicated that the MFA "regarded publication of the protest route map, drawn by the organisers of the illegal event, as an act encouraging participation and a call to action, which constitutes an attempt to interfere in Russia's domestic affairs" (Ministry of Foreign Affairs of the Russian Federation, "Comment by the Information and Press Department on the Demarche Presented to the US Embassy," webpage, August 9, 2019). Russia also expelled diplomats from Sweden, Poland, and Germany who were identified as participants of street protests in January 2021 (Ministry of Foreign Affairs of the Russian Federation, "Ob ob"yavlenii 'persona non grata" sotrudnikov diplomaticheskikh predstavitel'stv Shvetsii, Pol'shi i Germanii," webpage, February 5, 2021).

Duma elections. Putin criticized her for weighing in on the quality of the election before international observers reported their findings. He said she "gave a signal" to the opposition, who "heard the signal and began actively working with the help of the State Department."[61] Although this list is not exhaustive, it shows that Russian grievances regarding political interference are, in a sense, much broader than Western ones, although some overlap.

Comparison of Grievances

This analysis demonstrates that the grievances of the parties differ significantly. Russia's broader understanding of unacceptable interference encompasses several activities—such as funding NGOs—that Western governments believe to be well within the bounds of acceptable practices. However, some concerns of the United States, the EU, and Russia overlap. These include

- cyberattacks on election infrastructure
- public release of illicitly obtained information that has an impact on political processes
- activities of state-funded, foreign-language broadcasters
- use of social media to influence domestic politics.[62]

In our discussions, we sought to identify proposals to address these common grievances. Solutions to concerns that are not shared could be devised in principle, but they would likely entail asymmetric commitments or trade-offs. We focused instead on measures that would be applied equally to all parties.

---

[61] "Putin obvinyaet SShA v provotsirovanii protestov," *BBC Russian Service*, December 8, 2011.

[62] The foreign financing of political organizations and individuals is also a shared concern among the parties. However, our group did not have the opportunity to discuss it in detail.

CHAPTER THREE

Proposed Measures

This text was finalized in January 2022 and has not been subsequently revised.

Our discussions focused on reaching acceptable compromises between Russia and the West on possible measures to address the interference challenge. We did not attempt to find measures that would eliminate *all* behaviors that one side or another found objectionable. Instead, we sought to outline potentially mutually acceptable measures to curb *some* problematic activities, proscribe others, and provide a degree of mutual reassurance. We also tried to identify certain behaviors that *should be* acceptable and therefore not subject to further restrictions. Again, these proposals are not intended to be comprehensive; they reflect our discussions and our focus on finding compromise. Some of the contributors had reservations about some of these proposals; these reservations are discussed in greater detail at the end of this chapter and in Appendix B.

The divergences in the parties' grievances raise difficulties but also create options for negotiating potential agreements. For example, if one state conducts foreign influence campaigns on social media but another does not, measures to address those campaigns would have an asymmetric effect on those states. Such a scenario is relatively commonplace in international politics; several international agreements contain provisions that apply to all parties but affect the parties differently. Only the United States had ground-launched cruise missiles before it signed the Intermediate-Range Nuclear Forces Treaty, which banned them, and thus the treaty resulted in the destruction of only one party's ground-launched cruise missiles (both sides had intermediate-range ballistic missiles). There also are accords, such as the Iran nuclear deal, that impose different requirements on the respective parties as an effective quid pro quo. Another possibility is to agree on coordinated, parallel unilateral measures that address different concerns; for example, one party can stop a certain activity in return for the other party stopping a different one.

In short, divergences in states' grievances—and their political systems, international modus operandi, and capabilities—do not a priori rule out coming to an agreement; indeed, such divergences could create trade space in a negotiation. The measures proposed below emerged, in part, from the trade spaces that were identified in our discussions. However, rather than propose explicit quid pro quos, our group decided it would be best to focus on measures that the United States, Russia, and the EU could all adopt, with the understanding that their impact on the parties would differ. Such universal measures might be easier to agree to than trades would be. A state might be reluctant to give up an activity it sees as legitimate in return for another state's commitment to end a practice the first views as illegitimate. Equally, a state might be more inclined to agree not to engage in certain activities if it does so in a bilateral or multilateral context; a unilateral commitment might be seen as an admission of guilt.

The description of each proposed measure below is followed by a table summarizing the status quo and the proposed change.

Proposal 1: Increase Transparency Regarding Interpretations of Prohibited Interference

Our group extensively discussed definitions of the term *interference*. Coming to a shared definition of interference was seen by some group members as a prerequisite to discussing measures to address interference. After all, we needed to define the scope of our effort. The same prerequisite would likely arise in the context of intergovernmental talks on the subject. And the challenge of defining the term is far more than semantic. If interference is unacceptable, any activity deemed an example of interference becomes taboo. So, accepting a broad definition implies broad limitations on behavior. The definition also determines the scope of the negotiations. Differences between states on the definition of interference—specifically, what is or should be prohibited—reflect broader divergences in their political systems, international modus operandi, etc.

A key challenge is to distinguish between cases of unacceptable interference and activities of legitimate foreign policy, such as public diplomacy or engagement with the political opposition, that do not violate international law or applicable national laws—even if such activities are not necessarily welcomed by other governments. Russia and Western states have different views on what activities are prohibited under international law, reflecting a broader lack of consensus on where the line falls between acceptable and unacceptable behavior.[1]

Several components of international law can be applied to the issue of interference: most importantly, the prohibition on nonforcible intervention and human rights law. The customary international law prohibition on nonforcible intervention signifies the commitment of states not to intervene in matters that are essentially under the domestic jurisdiction of another state. The International Court of Justice has held that the element of coercion must be present to invoke the prohibition.[2] Subsequent Western interpretations have held that the coercion criterion effectively excludes most cases of political interference from the scope of the prohibition. In stark contrast to this narrow interpretation, another reading, often associated with Russia and other countries that emphasize national sovereignty, proposes a much broader understanding of the prohibition on nonforcible intervention. Russian legal scholars have argued that the UN Charter bars nearly all external attempts to intervene in a state's domestic affairs.[3] As a result of these divergent readings of the prohibition on nonforcible intervention, there is

---

[1] The discussion and recommendations in this paper would not prejudice ongoing multilateral processes and concrete measures that have been agreed among states already. The recommendations could usefully supplement those processes and measures.

[2] "[T]he element of coercion . . . defines, and indeed forms the very essence of, prohibited intervention" (International Court of Justice, Military and Paramilitary Activities in and Against Nicaragua [Nicaragua v. United States of America], Merits, Judgment, I.C.J. Reports 1986, para. 205).

[3] Aleksandr Vylegzhanin and Kirill Kritskii, "Souchastie SShA v gosudarstvennom perevorote v Kieve 2014 goda - eto mezhdunarodnoe pravonarushenie," *Mezhdunarodnaya zhizn'*, No. 3, 2019. Vylegzhanin and Kritskii cite Article 2(7), which states, "Nothing contained in the present Charter shall authorize the United Nations to intervene in matters which are essentially within the domestic jurisdiction of any state." Western scholars and governments have held that this prohibition relates only to actions of the UN itself, not its member states.

no international consensus, as Chimène Keitner notes, on "what tools short of force remain lawfully at states' disposal to pursue their foreign policy goals, particularly when those goals implicate the internal decision-making processes of other states."[4]

The prohibition on intervention pertains, first and foremost, to the actions of states. Matters pertaining to individuals or groups often fall (additionally) under the purview of international human rights law. Russia's sovereignty-centric interpretation of the prohibition on intervention suggests an all-encompassing authority of the state over affairs within its territory; other international norms do not give foreign actors the prerogative to limit that authority, unless authorized to do so by the UN Security Council. In contrast, the Western reading of international law partially subordinates the nonintervention norm to human-rights norms (and, correspondingly, provides for a generous latitude of the privilege to defend them).[5]

Given these divergent interpretations, international law is unlikely to provide the basis for determining the line between acceptable and unacceptable behavior. A focused dialogue among states about their respective views on the line between acceptable and unacceptable behavior, in both international and domestic law and as a matter of foreign policy—could increase common understanding and reduce the likelihood of miscalculation. Therefore, we recommend two ways that states could increase transparency regarding their respective approaches:

- The EU, Russia, and the United States should exchange information about their respective understandings of interference, including the

---

[4] Chimène I. Keitner, "Foreign Election Interference and International Law," in Duncan B. Hollis and Jens David Ohline, eds., *Defending Democracies: Combating Foreign Election Interference in a Digital Age*, New York: Oxford University Press, 2021, p. 187.

[5] See, for example, the Russian and Western government positions in UN, Official Compendium of Voluntary Contributions on the Subject of How International Law Applies to the Use of Information and Communications Technologies by States Submitted by Participating Governmental Experts in the Group of Governmental Experts on Advancing Responsible State Behavior in Cyberspace in the Context of International Security Established Pursuant to General Assembly Resolution 73/266, A/76/136, July 13, 2021.

types of activities that they consider unacceptable. If possible, such information would go beyond specific examples and include an articulation of the characteristics of unacceptable interference.

- Equally important, parties should outline what activities they *do not* consider to constitute interference. In other words, what activities should not be considered unacceptable?[6]

It can be argued that certain states benefit from the current ambiguity and lack of consensus about what is acceptable interference and what is not. But there is perhaps a stronger case to be made that such benefits are far outweighed by the negative consequences of the current tensions stemming from interference. Greater clarity on national positions would not tie the hands of any party but could assist in mitigating the severity of the interference problem. Greater transparency would allow the parties to understand each other's red lines and thus would help the parties avoid unintended escalation and miscalculation.

Proposal 1a: Consider Developing a Shared Set of Characteristics Associated with Unacceptable Interference

Providing greater transparency on national positions would be an important first step. But it would remain difficult to have a dialogue about specific cases of alleged interference because of the normative connotation of the term *interference*. Because, by definition, acts of interference could be construed as inherently contrary to international law, states have a strong incentive to categorically deny their involvement in such acts. Indeed, that certainly is the case today.

Therefore, in addition to greater transparency, states could consider developing a common set of characteristics associated with unacceptable acts of interference. This diagnostic approach, which would focus on the

---

[6] Some definitions of acceptable behaviors have already been proposed. For example, the DETER Act, which was under consideration in the U.S. Congress, excluded state-funded broadcasting from its definition of unacceptable behavior (Defending Elections Against Trolls from Enemy Regimes [DETER] Act, S. 1328, 116th Congress, 2019).

traits of a given event rather than broader international norms and principles, might offer Russia and the West a tool for discussing or even jointly addressing cases considered to be interference by any of the parties without invoking international legal issues or requiring a mutually accepted definition.

We provide an example of characteristics that states could consider in Appendix A. The more of these characteristics an action or event has, the more likely it is to be considered an example of unacceptable interference. Judgments about an activity can be made according to the characteristics that it demonstrates. Of course, such a diagnostic approach would be unnecessary for blatant acts of overt, hostile, clearly intentional, openly state-sponsored attempts to affect another state's political processes. But most cases of alleged interference are much more ambiguous. Developing a common diagnostic vocabulary could be less problematic than hammering out a shared definition of interference, since the former would not necessarily invoke the known international legal and normative disagreements among the parties. It could allow states to raise concerns about specific activities without implicitly accusing another party of violating a norm or accepting another party's assessment that a specific activity crosses the line. The diagnostic approach could also help a party to understand what specific activities other parties would regard as prohibited interference.

States have pursued similar efforts in other international contexts, and such definitions have had important consequences for national security. For example, the P5 process, a consultation format used by the five permanent members of the UN Security Council and launched by the 2010 Nuclear Non-Proliferation Treaty Review Conference, produced a multilingual glossary of nuclear terms in 2015.[7] Although some disarmament proponents have criticized the glossary, arguing that it has not bridged the major known definitional divides,[8] the process has been useful to the participants

---

[7] P5 Working Group on the Glossary of Key Nuclear Terms, *P5 Glossary of Key Nuclear Terms*, Beijing: China Atomic Energy Press, April 2015.

[8] Maximilian Hoell, "The P5 Process: Ten Years On," London: European Leadership Network, September 2019.

to reduce uncertainty and increase mutual understanding, even if just about the areas of disagreement.[9]

Table 3.1 summarizes the current state of mutual understanding among the parties and how our proposal would change it.

Proposal 2: Enhance Dialogue on Interference

In addition to enhanced transparency on their respective understandings of interference, Russia, the United States, and the EU should establish channels for regular dialogue to allow for more regular communication about these issues. The following specific measures could be considered:

- Establish high-level points of contact (PoCs) with responsibility for international engagement on the issue of foreign interference. At the moment, there is no single official in any government with the authority to engage internationally on the range of issues that are relevant to interference. The PoC's role should be given as an additional portfolio to a senior government official. This PoC would be responsible both for conveying concerns about other states' activities and for receiving and delegating concerns raised by other states.
- Commit publicly to respond to other parties' requests for clarification or additional information when concerns are raised through the PoCs,

TABLE 3.1

Mutual Understandings Status Quo and Proposed Change

Status Quo	Proposed Change
Not only do Russia and the West have different understandings of prohibited interference, but they also do not have clarity on where the other side draws the line.	• The EU, Russia, and the United States exchange information about their understandings of what activities they do and *do not* consider to be prohibited interference. • The parties consider developing a common diagnostic set of characteristics associated with unacceptable acts of interference.

---

[9] As one P-5 official stated, "The most interesting part of the glossary work is not the document per se. It is what is not in it. The terms we cannot agree on. This helps a lot in better understanding each other's perspective and has spin-off benefits for other work areas" (quoted in Hoell, 2019, p. 5).

to the extent allowed by domestic and international law. Whole-of-government buy-in is crucial, given the cross-cutting nature of interference. For example, financial authorities would be involved in cases involving foreign sources of funding. A party would be able to raise concerns according to its understanding of prohibited or problematic interference; another party need not adopt that same understanding to respond to the inquiry. Such a commitment could help ensure the utility of the PoC mechanism for the parties.

For states to engage seriously in such regular dialogue, they will need assurance that others will not resort to accusations of interference without prior consultation through these channels. Accusations of interference made publicly and without prior intergovernmental discussions can raise tensions and often do not result in changes in behavior. Therefore, the proposed dialogue mechanisms should be supported by clear commitments to engage before any accusation is made publicly. Such mechanisms would neither affect the states' rights and obligations under existing international law nor preclude the states from subsequently publicizing any allegations. Thus, the following additional measures could be considered:

- Commit to refraining from raising accusations about interference by another party without seeking clarification first through the aforementioned communication channels.
- Establish a dispute resolution mechanism that can be activated to address cases in which the commitment to respond is not upheld, the information provided by the designated PoCs is deemed insufficient or unsatisfactory, or a state goes public before consulting.

As noted above, "naming and shaming" would still be a policy option after engaging at an intergovernmental level. And if the consultation mechanisms prove unproductive, the parties could always decide to walk away from them and their related commitments. None of these mechanisms would stop a state that is determined to cross another's red lines. But they could raise the costs of doing so and thus create stronger disincentives than exist today.

For cases in which nonstate actors operating from the territory of one of the parties perpetrate interference activities that are illegal under the laws of another government, that government can still activate these communication channels to request assistance. Concrete and observable actions that bring perpetrators of interference to justice can build confidence in the effectiveness of the dialogue.[10]

Table 3.2 summarizes the status quo regarding communication channels and how we propose to improve on it.

Proposal 3: Establish Self-Restraint Commitments

We propose that the United States, the EU, and Russia commit *not* to undertake two activities that they all would agree to be unacceptable: (1) tampering with the mechanics of elections and (2) disclosing politically sensitive information obtained covertly.

Allegations of tampering with the mechanics of elections—that is, using cyber or other means to modify vote counts, compromise the integrity or perceived integrity of voting or vote counting or auditing systems, altering voter registration databases, denying service to those databases, etc.—

TABLE 3.2

Communication Channels Status Quo and Proposed Change

Status Quo	Proposed Change
No single official in any government has the authority to engage internationally on the range of issues that are relevant to interference.	• High-level PoCs for international engagement on foreign interference. • Public commitments to respond through the PoCs when concerns are raised. • Commitment to seek clarification through the PoCs before going public with accusations. • Dispute resolution mechanism to address concerns about the functioning of this channel.

---

[10] It is safe to assume that Europe and the United States would not assist when requests about nonstate actors would target political opposition or critics operating from their territories, if such activities are not considered illegal under domestic law. And Russia (as well as France and Germany) does not extradite its citizens under its constitution. However, effective communication on these matters could help prevent misunderstandings and misinterpretations.

are particularly explosive. Although there is no evidence of such tampering having taken place to date in Russia, the United States, or the EU, there have been reports of successful attempts to penetrate election-related infrastructure.[11] And all parties have raised concerns about the possibility of cyber intrusions into systems involved in elections.

Alleged *hack-and-leak operations*, whereby information of a politically sensitive nature in one country is made public after having been obtained by another state's (or its proxies') covert actions, have had a major deleterious impact on politics in several countries. States should commit to a norm that information pertaining to an ongoing political process in one country that is obtained covertly by a government or government-affiliated organization of another country should not be made public.

The most feasible form for undertaking such commitments could be coordinated statements issued separately by the respective parties. A joint statement might be preferable, but the wording could prove impossible to negotiate.

Some might object that only states that have engaged in these behaviors should undertake commitments not to do so in the future. However, such an approach would essentially require an admission of guilt, which no state is likely to make. Moreover, it costs states nothing to commit not to do something if they have not engaged, and do not plan to engage, in such activities.

Such commitments, regardless of the forms in which they are made, would not be ironclad guarantees. Instead, they would set standards and allow for greater accountability in case of violations. They would therefore raise the cost of violations, which could alter the decisionmaking calculus of those considering such a step.

Table 3.3 summarizes the current lack of commitments to self-restraint and our proposals to create them.

---

[11] U.S. Senate Select Committee on Intelligence, undated a.

TABLE 3.3
Self-Restraint Status Quo and Proposed Change

Status Quo	Proposed Change
No explicit commitment not to engage in two highly problematic activities: tampering with elections infrastructure and disclosing politically sensitive information obtained covertly.	• Coordinated statements that commit parties not to tamper with election mechanics and not to disclose politically sensitive information obtained covertly.

Proposal 4: Develop Technical Measures to Demonstrate Compliance with Self-Restraint Commitments

Of course, neither Russia nor the West would trust each other to comply with these two self-restraint commitments. Therefore, additional technical measures could be useful to implement both commitments and demonstrate compliance with them in the cyber domain. Although noncyber means can be employed to tamper with elections or obtain politically sensitive information covertly, the use of cyber means is far cheaper and less risky and thus more commonplace. The cyber domain also offers distinct opportunities for states to communicate and demonstrate adherence to commitments.

A basic precondition for the commitments to function effectively in the cyber domain is clarity as to which systems should be subject to them. Ambiguity on this question would devalue the commitments, since neither a potential attacker nor a defender can be sure when a red line is crossed.

Our proposal is to use technical measures to reduce ambiguity while avoiding key pitfalls. Specifically, offensive teams are not likely to take steps that put them at additional risk of discovery or attribution, and defensive teams would be averse to measures that could highlight critical infrastructure to potential attackers. It will be challenging to devise measures that boost confidence and avoid these challenges, but if it is possible to thread this needle, the benefits could be significant.

First, as a possible technical measure to support the norm of non-tampering with election infrastructure, states could use a mutually agreed-upon, limited number of digital cryptographic markers, or *tokens*, to label systems that they consider subject to the norm.[12] Each state could implant one of these cryptographically secured tokens onto a specified number of computer systems involved in relevant activities (e.g., elections). The tokens would be emplaced in such a way that they would definitely be visible to any intruder, but only those intruders privy to the arrangement (i.e., those working for one of the parties) would understand the token's meaning and be able to verify its authenticity.

These tokens would be small (in terms of bytes), nonforgeable, tied to particular systems or placement locations within those systems (e.g., by hashing the computer name and unique MAC address and signing it with a private key), and seemingly innocuous to parties not privy to the agreement. The states party to the measure would have strong incentives to keep the technical details of the tokens confidential from the public (and other states) so as to prevent false-flag operations.[13] The parties to such an agreement would be allocated an equal number of these tokens, using an agreed-upon format and mechanism for distribution.

The purpose of limiting the number of tokens would be to prevent one side from declaring all its systems off-limits. Doing so would undermine the integrity of the scheme, since its purpose is to cover only the most sensitive systems.

Some examples of techniques to ensure an attacker would naturally come across these tokens could include putting them in useful mail spools, password databases, known file locations on disks, or other data that an attacker would normally pull back or access for operational reasons. If sufficiently small, the tokens could be deployed in such areas as the comment fields of the election devices (i.e., vote-counting machines); the tabulation and reporting equipment that is used to count, verify, and communicate the voting results; or the networking equipment that connects the two. The tokens could also be placed on computers used by electoral officials.

Attackers from the states party to this measure would agree to actively search for these tokens in any data they pull back or view. Should an attacker

---

[12] This proposal would not preclude states from using their existing digital forensic tools and intelligence capabilities to investigate a suspected incident.

[13] The cryptographic security (also known as a *public/private key pair*) would also complicate false-flag operations.

encounter a token, the agreement would specify a set of actions to demonstrate compliance with the self-restraint norm. For example, parties would agree to immediately cease further intrusions and remove implants from the affected machine. The attacker would also have the option to inform the targeted state of the incident through specified confidential channels. (In most cases, the attacker's compliance with the norm will be visible during forensic activities undertaken by the defender.) The tokens thus allow for the defender to communicate red lines unambiguously and for the attacker to demonstrate compliance with the self-restraint norm clearly and avoid misunderstandings or misinterpretations.

The parties to this arrangement would have a shared interest in preventing the tokens from becoming targets for nonstate attackers or those from states not party to the arrangement. Therefore, the tokens would be designed to look innocuous to an attacker not familiar with the details of the agreement. Another way to prevent third-party attackers from using the tokens to identify high-value systems would be to make tokens signed with incorrect keys look similar to the "real" tokens and to place these "fake" tokens on noncritical systems. (Only the parties to the agreement would be able to distinguish between correct and incorrect keys.) As an additional security measure, genuine tokens would not be placed anywhere they could be discovered by public scanning activities.

This proposed measure would not require the parties to agree to a list of locations where the tokens could be placed. The tokens instead would serve as a means of communicating that wherever they are, the state has established a red line. The clear indication that a particular system is of high sensitivity and thus subject to the self-restraint norm would offer the opportunity for a potential intruding party to reaffirm compliance with the norm through visible behaviors and established communication procedures.

It is a feature of this proposal that no agreement would be necessary regarding which systems would be critical enough to deserve a token. Each side could distribute its tokens wherever it saw fit. This approach would allow for the divergences among the parties resulting from the peculiarities of their political systems. Avoiding an intractable definitional argument over which systems would be part of critical election infrastructure and which would not is a key advantage of this proposal.

Determining the technical details of this proposal, including how to determine the number of tokens for each side, would be the subject of future negotiations among the governments. We have outlined a framework for clearly demonstrating red lines and communicating compliance with those red lines to operationalize the norm of nontampering with election systems. This framework allows the states to avoid seeking agreement on which systems or even types of systems should be considered high-risk or off-limits for certain offensive cyber exploitations.

Given the current lack of trust among the potential parties to this proposal, it would make sense to roll out this measure gradually. The parties could start with municipal or local elections as a pilot or proof of concept. If the parties are satisfied with the others' compliance, the parties could employ the measure in regional and then national elections. If successful, such a gradual roll-out would build confidence in the scheme's viability and the parties' compliance with it. If the states fail to comply, the parties could pull out of the arrangement.

Second, the commitment to nondisclosure of politically sensitive information obtained covertly could be monitored through a similar token-based approach. Governments could mark the systems used by politically sensitive individuals and institutions with a similar digital cryptographic token scheme. Again, the technical details of these tokens would be known only to the governments that would be party to the scheme. The number of tokens could also be limited, particularly during the first stages of implementation.

These tokens for politically sensitive information would convey a different message from those related to election infrastructure. Rather than demarcating a boundary that government attackers should not cross, the nondisclosure tokens would proscribe neither network exploitation nor even exfiltration of information by attackers. Instead, these tokens would convey a warning to the effect that leaking any information obtained from this mailbox or system would be considered a violation of the agreed-upon norm of nondisclosure of covertly obtained politically sensitive information. Given the nature of this norm, the attacker would not communicate with the defender following the discovery of the token. But there would be no ambiguity about the attacker's intentions if the information were leaked.

Even if both measures were successfully implemented, states could still choose how to act, and the token schemes would not prevent them from violating the self-restraint commitments. But the advantage of this proposal is that it would establish clear red lines, minimize the chances of miscalculation and misunderstanding, and, if observed, allow for mutual reassurance. If a state deliberately attacked a designated piece of protected election infrastructure or leaked information from a designated individual despite the presence of the tokens, there could be no doubt that such a step would be a deliberate escalation, because a state could not credibly assert that it did not know the exploited systems were covered by the norm.

Table 3.4 summarizes our proposal to create mechanisms for communicating compliance with the self-restraint norms.

Proposal 5: Create Guidelines to Limit Cross-Border Manipulation of Social Media

Social media platforms have become central to politics in many countries. Given their inherent permeability, these platforms have become a particularly effective medium for influence operations, including those allegedly conducted by one state to affect the political processes of another. There have been numerous accounts of organized influence campaigns targeting the citizens of one country that originated outside of that country. These operations are low cost, and state involvement in their execution can be made plausibly deniable by outsourcing their implementation to contractors or other nonstate actors. Indeed, persistent state-sponsored attempts at "cross-border" interference via social media seem to be the new normal.

State-sponsored influence campaigns are, by definition, covert; no state has yet admitted to conducting or sponsoring them. Given the public deni-

TABLE 3.4

Self-Restraint Compliance Status Quo and Proposed Change

Status Quo	Proposed Change
Even if the self-restraint norms were agreed to, neither Russia nor the West would know which systems are covered by them.	• Digital "tokens" to label election systems subject to the norm, and established procedures for what to do should a token be discovered. • Tokens for politically significant organizations and individuals to clarify the implementation of the nondisclosure norm.

als and the involvement of nonstate proxies and contractors, this problem would be very difficult—if not impossible—to address through international negotiations among governments about the conduct of the governments themselves. Moreover, criminal prosecutions in domestic courts do not seem to be viable alternatives; states either cannot or will not extradite suspects, and defendants can abuse the discovery process.[14]

However, social media companies could minimize the effect of state-sponsored cross-border influence campaigns by changing their practices. In the past, social media companies have implemented such changes in response both to domestic laws and regulations in the countries where they operate and to less-formalized guidance from the political sphere, such as public outcry or political consensus. Our proposal is for the EU, the United States, and Russia to consider coordinating a set of recommended guidelines to social media companies for an effective, consistent, and transparent approach that would limit the impact of cross-border influence campaigns on the platforms. In some jurisdictions, these guidelines could be implemented through local or national laws and regulations, but the social media companies would likely welcome multilaterally agreed-upon, consistent guidelines on this matter and could implement them voluntarily without new formal legal requirements. Indeed, some social media companies have openly called for exactly such an effort.[15]

Social media companies do have significant technical capacity to filter and moderate content on their platforms. The companies are extremely vigilant about rooting out child abuse material.[16] They filter Islamic State of Iraq and Syria (ISIS) propaganda.[17] They filter things differently in different countries because of the distinct legal environments in different states. To comply with German law, Twitter blocks access to certain far-right content

---

[14] Sarah N. Lynch, "U.S. Prosecutors Drop Mueller-Era Case Against Russian Firm," *Reuters*, March 16, 2020.

[15] Mark Zuckerberg, "The Internet Needs New Rules. Let's Start in These Four Areas," *Washington Post*, March 30, 2019.

[16] Charles Arthur, "Twitter to Introduce PhotoDNA System to Block Child Abuse Images," *The Guardian*, July 22, 2013; and Catherine Smith, "Facebook Adopts Microsoft PhotoDNA to Remove Child Pornography," *HuffPost*, July 20, 2011.

[17] Twitter, "Combating Violent Extremism," *Twitter Blog*, February 5, 2016.

for users in Germany, but the same content is freely available to users in the United States.[18] The platforms also have the technical capacity to distinguish between humans and bots—at least in many cases.[19]

For information on social media to have a political effect on a given polity, it must reach a critical mass of viewers. This reach is often referred to as *trending*. In practice, trending can occur either *organically* or through *artificial amplification*. Content can spread widely across borders and shift the landscape of trending topics organically if there is enough natural interest—for example, during major international events, such as the World Cup or the Olympics. The guidelines proposed here are not intended to alter such organic trends, and it would be important for social media companies to avoid inadvertently doing so.

In contrast, artificial amplification refers to the process of directly and intentionally causing a topic or narrative to trend in excess of the organic interest in the topic. Amplification can be done legitimately by paying a social media company directly to promote an ad or other content, or it can be done illegitimately by using such techniques as botnets and cyborgs, which often (but not always) violate the platforms' terms of service. Propaganda and political influence campaigns require heavy use of nonorganic amplification because their purpose is to affect their targets' beliefs and emotions. In other words, only content that is artificially amplified can influence a large enough audience to be effective at political influence.[20]

If social media platforms attempted to limit what content could be transmitted, retweeted, etc. according to subject matter (e.g., in favor of a specific candidate) or place of origin (e.g., Americans retweeting information

---

[18] Mikayla Appell, "A New Responsibility for Internet Platforms: Germany's New Hate Speech Law," American Institute for Contemporary Germany Studies, January 23, 2018.

[19] Jack Nicas, "Why Can't the Social Networks Stop Fake Accounts?" *New York Times*, December 8, 2020. See also Yoel Roth, "Because of this, API-based research can't distinguish between accounts we've already identified as bad (and hidden or removed) and real, authentic ones," Twitter post, November 2, 2018; and Yoel Roth, "Information Operations on Twitter: Principles, Process, and Disclosure," *Twitter Blog*, June 13, 2019, for a discussion of how Twitter can identify inauthentic accounts more reliably than independent researchers can.

[20] Gregory Asmolov, "The Effects of Participatory Propaganda: From Socialization to Internalization of Conflicts," *Journal of Design and Science*, August 7, 2019.

from Russia), that could pose undue limitations on freedom of speech and expression, especially if such limitations were imposed as a result of pressure by governments. Furthermore, although states do not generally guarantee free speech to foreign states or individuals, a "great firewall" approach of comprehensively censoring information from outside a state's borders would be highly undesirable. Yet, a middle ground of limiting the ability of *foreign* actors to artificially amplify content could minimize the impact of foreign influence campaigns on social media platforms without restricting free speech.[21]

Some social media companies have taken steps to limit foreign influence campaigns, such as shutting down foreign-funded or foreign-operated networks of bots or banning foreign accounts that consistently participate in deceptive, inflammatory, or abusive activities focused on politics or elections. Twitter, Facebook, and YouTube all cracked down on non-U.S. accounts allegedly engaged in influence campaigns inside the United States, and most social media companies' terms of service explicitly prohibit such activity.[22]

But until quite recently, no platform has had a clear and transparent set of policies to counter cross-border political interference. The policies that do exist, while certainly an improvement, were implemented only because of significant public outcry and widespread belief that harm had already occurred. Enforcement continues to be inconsistent, since either relevant decisions or the design of automated algorithms to make those decisions rely on subjective judgments of the social media companies' platform integrity teams. The countermeasures implemented thus far are applied differently according to the country from which the content originates and the countries at which the content is targeted. Furthermore, because these efforts all are voluntary self-regulation, there is nothing preventing the social media companies from scaling them back as soon as public attention shifts—or because of a change in leadership. Addressing cross-border

---

[21] Of course, there are a variety of other problems relating to foreign political interference via social media, such as microtargeting of specific groups.

[22] For example, Meta, "Inauthentic Behavior," webpage, undated; Meta, "Preparing for Elections," webpage, 2021; Twitter, "Civic Integrity Policy," webpage, October 2021; and YouTube, "Our Commitments: Supporting Political Integrity," webpage, undated.

artificial amplification would be a powerful counter to foreign influence campaigns on social media and could help minimize subjectivity in social media companies' decisionmaking and avoid origin-based discrimination. Focusing on limits on amplification would also avoid more-draconian measures, such as account bans or complete content blocking, and thus account for free speech concerns.

Therefore, we recommend that the EU, the United States, and Russia consider agreeing to coordinated guidelines that would encourage social media platforms to limit *cross-border artificial amplification*: that is, deliberate attempts originating in one country to manipulate social media platform algorithms in order to promote particular content in another country. These guidelines would not require content blocking or even shutting down accounts. Instead, social media companies would prevent artificial attempts from outside a country to influence the growth of trends in that country.[23] The platforms would preclude content from being amplified by artificial activities emanating from another country. For example, networks of bots, cyborgs, and other inauthentic accounts operating out of Macedonia would not be allowed to affect the trending news seen in the Facebook newsfeeds of U.S. users.[24] In implementing such a plan, social media companies would face challenges in distinguishing cross-border organic trends from artificial trends, but it would be in their business interests to protect the organic trends.[25]

This proposal would involve neither governments nor social media companies in assessing the nature of online content to determine what might be political interference. By focusing on *all* cross-border artificial amplification, the measure would avoid the minefield of granting either private entities or states the power to determine what is "political" content and what is not. As a result, cross-border artificial amplification for commercial pur-

---

[23] This would, of course, also include ordinary paid political advertising originating outside the target country, although this is, for the most part, already not allowed.

[24] Andrew Byrne, "Macedonia's Fake News Industry Sets Sights on Europe," *Financial Times*, December 15, 2016.

[25] It is also in the business interest of the social media companies' advertising customers to be assured that their "clicks" are coming from real accounts rather than foreign bots, so that may be an additional source of support for such a plan.

poses (e.g., a company based in one country using botnets to promote its products on social media platforms in another) would also be curtailed. Such activity is already a violation of the social media platforms' terms of service. And cross-border promotion of commercial products through legal, paid advertising would not be affected by this measure.

States could agree to these guidelines at the international level, but the specific steps to implement them would depend on a given state's political, constitutional, and legal peculiarities. These steps could range from public exhortation to formal regulation. Many social media companies are U.S.-based (although Russia has its own domestic social networks, such as VKontakte), but the U.S. companies tend to comply with the laws and norms in the other states where they operate. Our proposed approach would delegate the tasks of verification and attribution to the social media platforms. The platforms would also be responsible for enforcement.

To implement this measure, the states would require some means of engaging with the social media companies. Most social media companies have government policy teams that provide PoCs to some governments. In other cases, lines of communication between governments and social media companies do not exist. Standardizing these lines of communication, by formalizing the existing ones and establishing new ones where necessary, would enable effective communication between the companies and governments.

Our proposal is essentially for an international call to encourage social media companies to construct major roadblocks to cross-border influence campaigns. It is similar in form to previous public-private initiatives, such as the Christchurch Call to Action.[26] Although any one state could adopt our proposal unilaterally, its political and practical impact would be more significant if the EU, the United States, and Russia were to adopt it.

This proposal neither prevents states from attempting social media influence campaigns in other countries nor obliges them not to do so. However, it stems from the premise that the social media companies have the

---

[26] The Christchurch Call to Action was a commitment by governments and tech companies, since the 2019 mosque shootings in Christchurch, New Zealand, to eliminate terrorist and violent extremist content online. See Christchurch Call, "Supporters," webpage, undated.

technical capacity (and, to some extent, a business incentive) to defuse this issue—or at least greatly mitigate it—regardless of whether states continue to sponsor such campaigns. Given the challenges associated with addressing this problem directly, our proposal offers a potential way forward. Of course, even if this proposal were agreed-upon and fully implemented, it would likely not completely eliminate cross-border state-sponsored influence campaigns on social media, but it could have a significant effect in ameliorating the problem.

Table 3.5 summarizes our proposal.

Proposal 6: Relax Restrictions on Foreign Broadcasters

Foreign broadcasting (that is, state-funded, foreign-language broadcasting) has increasingly played into debates about cross-border political interference. Officials and analysts in the United States, Russia, and the EU have accused foreign broadcasters of distributing propaganda, conducting influence campaigns, and favoring certain political forces.[27]

As a result, restrictions have been imposed on foreign broadcasters by the United States, Russia, and certain EU member states. Although such efforts to block foreign broadcasting predate the Cold War, we are witnessing what can be called a new arms race of regulation of foreign broadcasting

TABLE 3.5

Cross-Border Manipulation of Social Media Status Quo and Proposed Change

Status Quo	Proposed Change
Social media companies essentially determine when and how to address foreign influence campaigns and lack consistent, transparent, consistently enforced rules to prevent them.	• Internationally agreed-upon guidelines for social media companies to limit all cross-border artificial amplification.

---

[27] In this paper, we put to one side the question of the audience size for any of these media, from RT to the BBC. It is fair to say that, regardless of their audience sizes, these media play significant roles in the respective governments' threat perceptions regarding foreign interference.

in Russia, the United States, and (to a lesser extent) the EU. In other words, all parties are ratcheting up restrictions on these entities, at least partially in response to the other parties' restrictions. These regulations have severely complicated the work of foreign broadcasters.

In the United States, RT was compelled to register as a foreign agent under FARA, which imposed greater reporting requirements. RT journalists' access to Congress was also restricted.[28] In the EU, FARA-like registration is generally not required.[29] Most EU member states and European institutions oppose such requirements and point to the negative implications they might have for freedom of expression and democracy.[30] Although such normative reservations seem to persist, the growing concerns about disinformation campaigns and foreign interference in national elections are weakening them.[31] As part of their national media regulatory agendas, some EU member states have taken actions against specific foreign outlets, such as RT and Sputnik. In summer 2020, Latvia and Lithuania decided to ban television channels belonging to RT.[32] Estonia had done so half a year earlier. France acted against RT and Sputnik in 2017, when they were excluded from certain press events in the final phase of the presidential election campaign. In reaction to intelligence agencies' reports on the alleged meddling

---

[28] "RT America Stripped of Congress Credentials, While State Dept Says FARA Won't Change Its Status," *RT*, November 29, 2017.

[29] To strengthen democratic resilience against disinformation campaigns and interference, the EU has increased its activities. In December 2020, the EU presented regulations (such as the Digital Services Act) and action plans (such as the Action Plan on Democracy) that should help to protect media freedom and democratic discourse in the media. In 2021, the European Commission announced legislation on the transparency of sponsored political content.

[30] European Commission for Democracy Through Law, *On the Compatibility with International Human Rights Standards of a Series of Bills Introduced by the Russian State Duma Between 10 and 23 November 2020 to Amend Laws Affecting "Foreign Agents,"* Strasbourg, France, CDL-AD(2021)027, July 6, 2021.

[31] European Parliament, "Priority Question for Written Answer P-003967/2019: Russian Interference in European Democracies," November 21, 2019.

[32] Lauren Chadwick, "Lithuania Follows Latvia in Banning Russian Broadcaster RT," *Euronews*, July 9, 2020.

of foreign countries into the Brexit referendum in 2016, the UK government in 2020 proposed legislation inspired by the U.S. FARA law.

Russia passed its own Foreign Agents law in 2012, but only in 2019 was it amended to apply to media organizations.[33] The sponsors of the legislation said it was aimed at countering foreign interference into Russia's domestic politics.[34] Even before the passage of the legislation, RFE/RL and VOA had been forced off AM radio broadcasts throughout most of the country and had been confined to Internet-based media.[35] VOA, RFE/RL, and several of their affiliated media outlets have been designated foreign agents in recent years.[36] Once a news organization is designated a foreign agent, it must clearly state that designation on all its output. Severe financial and other penalties can be levied for noncompliance. RFE/RL, which has been designated under the law and has refused to register, has been assessed large fines and is facing the possible closure of its Russian operations.[37]

Many Western commentators have rejected any equivalence between RT on the one hand and RFE/RL, DW, and the BBC on the other. They argue that the latter have publicly visible and independent governance structures that shield editorial departments from government interference, whereas RT does not.[38] Even if these distinctions are accurate, they are unlikely to

---

[33] President of Russia, "V zakonodatel'stvo vneseny izmeneniya, kasayushchiesya inostrannykh SMI, vypolnyayushchikh funkstii inostrannogo agenta," December 2, 2019.

[34] Federation Council, "O massovom primenenii zakona ob inostrannykh agentakh v Rossii rechi ne idet – A. Klimov," webpage, December 9, 2020b.

[35] U.S. Agency for Global Media, "Russia Clamps Down Further on U.S. International Media," April 4, 2014.

[36] Ministry of Justice of the Russian Federation, "Vedenie reestra inostrannykh sredstv massovo informatsii vypolnyayushchikh funktsii inostrannogo agenta," webpage, June 11, 2020. DW is not on that list but has come under criticism from the State Duma (Ekaterina Venkina, "DW otvergaet ugrozy so storony Gosdumy," *Deutsche Welle*, September 4, 2019).

[37] "RSE/RS trebuet otmeny prikaza Roskomnadzora o SMI – 'inosagentakh,'" *Golos Ameriki*, June 3, 2021; and "'Radio Svoboda' oshtrafoval na 79 mln rublei za otsutsvie markirovki SMI-inoagenta," *TASS*, April 16, 2021.

[38] Justin Schlosberg, "In Search of Credibility: RT and the BBC in a 'Post-Truth' World," Foreign Policy Centre, March 21, 2017.

convince the relevant parties to change their behavior. Both Russia and Western governments believe the other side's entities are engaged in political interference. So what should be done?

The choice today is between a continual arms race of ever-greater regulation or a mutual disarmament process, which (in this case) means that all sides dial back regulation. We argue that states should exclude state-funded foreign broadcast media from their respective foreign agent laws, provided those media fully disclose their funding sources in ways that are visible and clear. After all, the original purpose of FARA registration was to establish transparency regarding influence activities conducted on behalf of foreign governments and other foreign entities. When it comes to news media, it is more important for the readers and viewers of content to have transparency about foreign government funding than it is for governments to have transparency about the activities of the operating corporations. Therefore, rather than applying foreign agent laws, governments should consider regulations that require the disclosure of foreign government funding for foreign broadcasters.

If the current trajectory of ever-greater restrictions on foreign broadcasters continues, both Russian state-sponsored foreign broadcasting in the West and Western state-sponsored foreign broadcasting in Russia might well cease operations. That outcome would be far more detrimental than whatever would be lost by waiving or repealing the FARA registration requirements.

The parties should recognize that their own efforts at foreign broadcasting imply that it is an acceptable activity, so long as full disclosure of state funding is made.[39] That does not mean accepting an equivalence among the different state-sponsored media. But it does mean acknowledging the reality that all parties are likely to impose ever-greater restrictions unless some mutual understanding is reached.

Table 3.6 summarizes the status quo regarding regulation of foreign broadcasters and our proposal.

---

[39] Covert funding, either of foreign broadcasting or of foreign-language web-based media, should certainly not be acceptable behavior.

TABLE 3.6

Foreign Broadcasting Status Quo and Proposed Change

	Status Quo	Proposed Change
United States	RT is forced to register as a foreign agent under FARA; most other foreign broadcasters are exempt.	• Regulations compelling full disclosure of funding sources for foreign broadcasters could replace FARA registration.
Russia	VOA and RFE/RL have been forced to register as foreign agents with onerous marking and reporting requirements, plus fines for noncompliance.	• Regulations compelling full disclosure of funding sources for foreign broadcasters could replace FARA registration.
EU	Some member states have tried to restrict or regulate Russian foreign broadcasters; others have not.	• EU-wide mandatory disclosure of funding sources could be coupled with a reversal of bans on foreign broadcasters in those countries that have imposed them.

Proposal 7: Formulate Declarations of Intent Not to Interfere

The United States, the EU, and Russia have all denied any intention to foment instability or to undermine the political systems of the other parties. For example, U.S. President Joe Biden has written, "Russia harbors an erroneous but stubborn—perhaps even obsessive—belief that Washington is actively pursuing regime change in Russia. There is no truth to that idea; the United States has never sought to remove Putin."[40] European leaders have echoed this sentiment.[41] And Putin has denied any desire to undermine the West.[42]

---

[40] Joseph R. Biden, Jr., and Michael Carpenter, "How to Stand Up to the Kremlin: Defending Democracy Against Its Enemies," *Foreign Affairs*, January/February 2018.

[41] European Commission, "EU-Russia Relations: Commission and High Representative Propose the Way Forward," press release, Brussels, June 16, 2021.

[42] "[It is] not our aim to divide anything or anybody in Europe. On the contrary, we want to see a united and prosperous European Union, because the European Union is our biggest trade and economic partner. The more problems there are within the European Union, the greater the risks and uncertainties for us" (President of Russia, "Interv'yu avstriiskomu telekanalu ORF," June 4, 2018).

Despite claiming the lack of such an intention vis-à-vis the other side, both Russia and the West allege that the other side is actively undermining its political system. This perception—that the objective of political interference is to *weaken* the targeted state from within, not merely to *influence* its political system—is particularly destabilizing, since it suggests deeply hostile intentions. It could therefore be politically significant for Russia and the West to accompany any agreement on the measures proposed above with declarations of the lack of intent to interfere.

In September 2020, Putin publicly proposed something similar: that the United States and Russia "exchange, in a mutually acceptable format, guarantees of non-intervention into internal affairs of each other, including into electoral processes, inter alia, by means of the ICTs [information and communication technologies] and high-tech methods."[43] However, this formulation could be problematic, given the parties' divergent understandings of the line between acceptable and unacceptable interference. Even if such guarantees were made, those divergent understandings would limit the practical impact of such an agreement.

As an alternative to an agreement, the parties could issue coordinated unilateral statements articulating their lack of intention to interfere, reaffirming their relevant international commitments (according to their respective national understandings thereof), and specifically disavowing efforts to foment instability or to undermine the political systems of the other parties. The latter, extreme form of interference is one that all parties should be able to agree to disavow, since, as noted above, both Russian and Western leaders have publicly done so in the past.

Such statements would be more specific than a general noninterference pledge and might provide a degree of both political reassurance and more-specific accountability. By making public commitments, the states could incur a higher cost for violating them. Although such a commitment in itself might not lead to immediate changes in behavior, it would be an important signal of intentions.

Table 3.7 summarizes our proposal.

---

[43] President of Russia, "Statement by President of Russia Vladimir Putin on a Comprehensive Program of Measures for Restoring the Russia-US Cooperation in the Field of International Information Security," September 25, 2020.

TABLE 3.7
Declarations of Intent Status Quo and Proposed Change

Status Quo	Proposed Change
Russian and Western leaders both allege that the other side is actively undermining its political system.	• Coordinated unilateral statements articulating a lack of intention to interfere, reaffirming existing international commitments, and specifically disavowing efforts to foment instability or to undermine the political systems of the other parties.

Reservations and Concerns from Contributors

The seven proposals outlined above represent the closest that the three groups of participants in our discussions could come to reaching consensus, but each of the three groups had remaining reservations and concerns about some of the proposals. Each group drafted a statement articulating their respective concerns. These statements appear in Appendix B. It is our hope that these statements will encourage further discussion and debate regarding these proposals.

CHAPTER FOUR

Summary and Conclusions

This text was finalized in January 2022 and has not been subsequently revised.

The EU, the United States, and Russia have divergent interests, values, and worldviews, as well as significant mutual grievances. Our contention is that, despite these divergences and grievances (and maybe *because* of the grievances), all parties would benefit from the establishment of mutually agreed-upon measures to mitigate the destabilizing impacts of political interference.

Our proposals are as follows:

1. Increase transparency regarding interpretations of prohibited interference.
2. Enhance dialogue on interference.
3. Establish self-restraint commitments (regarding election-related infrastructure and hack-and-leak operations).
4. Develop technical measures to demonstrate compliance with self-restraint commitments.
5. Create guidelines to limit cross-border manipulation of social media.
6. Relax restrictions on foreign broadcasters.
7. Formulate declarations of intent not to interfere.

The first two proposals could address the challenges created by the parties' divergent understandings of interference. Communication and dialogue are important mechanisms to reduce tensions and minimize the chances of miscalculation even among states that continue to disagree on core issues. The next two proposals—self-restraint commitments and related compliance measures—address two key shared grievances: possible attacks on election-related infrastructure and hack-and-leak operations. All sides also are concerned about external attempts to interfere in their politics via social media, and such attempts would be mitigated by the fifth proposal. As for the sixth proposal, the governments might not like the content of other states' foreign broadcasters, but the current arms race of greater restrictions seems to be leading to the shutdown of all parties' foreign broadcasting even though all parties implicitly accept it as a legitimate activity, since they all engage in it. Avoiding the complete cessation of foreign broadcasting in return for some mutual relaxations of restrictions, while maintaining full transparency regarding the funding sources of state-sponsored media, would be a better outcome. Finally, the proposed declarations of intent could contribute to both reassurance and public accountability.

If one or more of these proposals are agreed upon, a joint effort to monitor developments and issue a report on implementation after a specified period would be useful. The participants in this effort could include government, private sector, and civil society representatives. The report would not need to be consensus-based; if anything, it could clarify where major differences between the parties still lie.

Developing internationally agreed-upon measures to address political interference will continue to pose several challenges. Most significant, perhaps, is the reality that political interference between Russia and the West is seen as a tool in an ongoing geopolitical struggle. Some argue that the tool will be used as long as the struggle continues. Our contention is that both Russia and the West are concerned enough about interference that they may be willing to change certain behaviors so long as some of their respective concerns are addressed. It is at least worthwhile to test that proposition at the negotiating table. Doing so would require all parties to tacitly accept that even though past interference was intentional, states could be willing to choose not to engage in similar behavior—or at least to engage in substantially less of it—in the future.

International agreements to curb intentional—as opposed to unintentional or accidental—behavior have been successful in the past. In 1972, the United States (followed later by 11 other North Atlantic Treaty Organization [NATO] allies) and the Soviet Union signed the Incidents at Sea Agreement (INCSEA), which put in place mechanisms to prevent incidents on and over the high seas. Going into the talks on INCSEA, the U.S. side thought these incidents had resulted mostly from deliberate Soviet actions, even if the (rare) actual collisions had been unintended. Nonetheless, the U.S. side proposed to the Soviets a negotiation on "rules of the road" for governing future actions at sea, and those talks produced an agreement that is in force to this day.[1] Given this successful historical precedent, it is plausible to imagine the parties agreeing to a comparable set of rules of the road for limiting foreign interference.

Of course, INCSEA did not completely eliminate dangerous encounters between U.S. and Soviet/Russian ships and aircraft. Indeed, there has been an uptick in such incidents in recent years. But INCSEA established communication channels, standards of acceptable behavior, and mechanisms for demonstrating compliance (such as agreed-upon signaling codes between ships) and dramatically reduced the frequency and severity of these incidents, some of which had involved scores of casualties in the pre-INCSEA era. If international agreements regarding political interference were to have a similar effect—not eliminating the problem but mitigating it significantly—that would be a major step forward.

---

[1]   See David F. Winkler, *Incidents at Sea: American Confrontation and Cooperation with Russia and China, 1945–2016*, Annapolis, Md.: Naval Institute Press, 2017.

Sample Framework for a Diagnostic Approach to Defining Prohibited Interference

This text was finalized in January 2022 and has not been subsequently revised.

Agreement among the United States, the EU, and Russia on a definition of political interference is likely to prove impossible. However, it might be possible to agree to a list of characteristics associated with interference activities that are deemed unacceptable. This "diagnostic" approach might allow for a common understanding of problematic activities without crossing any political red lines.

The following outline provides an example of what a diagnostic definition might look like. It is essentially a list of characteristics associated with interference activities. No individual characteristic is decisive in determining whether a certain activity counts as interference. Some characteristics are unusual and rare, and others are very common, but they all add useful information. An interference *campaign* refers to a collection of activities (e.g., funding candidates or hacking emails) and artifacts (news articles, leaflets, social media posts, broadcasts, etc.) that are planned and coordinated by some entity toward a definable goal.[1]

Although no single characteristic here is determinative, some are more important than others.

---

[1] See Cognitive Security Collaborative, "AMITT Use Cases," webpage, March 11, 2021.

1. Government involvement characteristics
   a. Some or all campaign activities are conducted by a government or by an entity associated with or funded by a government.
   b. Individuals involved in the campaign have connections to government officials.
2. Campaign source, planning, and operation characteristics
   a. Campaign is operated from outside target country.
   b. Campaign is funded from outside target country.
   c. Campaign is planned or motivated by entities or individuals outside target country.
3. Content characteristics
   a. Content is related to political processes (such as an election) in target country.
   b. Content is oriented toward fomenting civil unrest in target country.
   c. Content advocates socially destructive (e.g., violent) or unhealthy (e.g., antivaccination) behavior or inflames intergroup tensions or conflicts.
   d. Content is factually and objectively untrue.
   e. Content uses emotionally or cognitively manipulative techniques.
4. Legal characteristics
   a. Campaign activities are illegal, according to the laws of the target state.
   b. Campaign incites activities that are illegal in the target state.
   c. Campaign activities lack explicit consent of the target state.
   d. The campaign uses, promotes, or amplifies content that was obtained illegally.
5. Characteristics of individuals involved in the campaign
   a. Individuals reside outside target country.
   b. Individuals located in target country are paid from sources outside target country.
6. Opacity and deception
   a. Operation location is misrepresented or hidden.
   b. Funding source is misrepresented or hidden.
   c. Efforts are made to misrepresent or hide government involvement.

7.   Characteristics specific to influence campaigns on social networks
     a.   There is use of fully automated accounts (bots).
     b.   There is use of partially automated accounts (cyborgs).
     c.   There is use of accounts operated by humans who misrepresent their identities (sock puppets).
     d.   There is use of accounts owned and/or operated by or on behalf of governments.
     e.   Targeting characteristics of influence campaign (direct, indirect, or inferred targeting)[2]
          i.   Targeting is based on identity or political party affiliation.
          ii.   Targeting is based on interest in political processes in target country (e.g., election fraud).
          iii. Targeting is based on interest in dissent or unrest in target country.
          iv.   Targeting is aimed at a narrowly defined social group.

---

[2] *Direct targeting* means the intended audience is explicitly known: for example, an ad campaign that is formally purchased from a social network or broadcast company requests a specific audience (such as likely partisan voters). *Indirect targeting* means targeting information is available, but the true target is obscured through the use of proxy characteristics, such as zip code or race (see, e.g., Alethea Lange and Rena Coen, "How Does the Internet Know Your Race?" Center for Democracy and Technology, September 7, 2016). *Inferred targeting* means there is no explicit list of targeting criteria available: for example, the targeting of an illicit botnet may be inferred only through statistical analysis of observed artifacts and how they are propagated.

Contributors' Reservations and Concerns

This text was finalized in January 2022 and has not been subsequently revised.

Statement by the U.S. Contributors[1]

The U.S. group believes this document represents a significant step forward toward possible agreed-upon international measures to address the interference issue. We have concerns about the viability of the proposals in the current political climate, both inside the United States and among the states concerned. The politics of negotiating with Moscow are always challenging; doing so regarding such a charged issue makes them even more treacherous. Even if both Russia and the West agree to the proposals, their effectiveness will depend on the political will of all the parties to change the behavior of state and nonstate actors within their respective jurisdictions. If an international agreement such as the one proposed here would generate the political will to do so, that would be a major achievement. Furthermore, we note that the proposals leave unchanged certain U.S. policies, such as democracy promotion and the internet freedom agenda, which many believe to be significant irritants to the Kremlin. It therefore remains an open question whether the proposals would provide Russia with enough incentive

---

[1] This text was written before the events of February 2022; in the environment that now prevails, a collaborative project like this would have been impossible. In order to share the ideas generated by our project but avoid any possible challenges for the contributors, we have decided to withhold their names.

to curtail the most significant irritants to the United States. Certainly, it is worth a try; moreover, such an attempt is the only way to find out. Finally, Proposal 5 ("create guidelines to limit cross-border manipulation of social media") could be a challenge for the United States to implement. Although the major social media companies are headquartered in the United States, the U.S. government faces severe legal and political constraints on influencing their activities. Moreover, even nonbinding guidelines for the social media platforms that might be agreed to with Russia would be subject to criticism and political resistance *precisely because* they were agreed to with Russia, regardless of their content.

Statement by the European Union Contributors[2]

The EU contributors have four main concerns about the final text. First, this project has been based on two assumptions: (1) that addressing the challenge of interference in a mutually acceptable way could help to stabilize the relationship between Russia and the West and (2) that an effective solution to this problem will require concerned states to agree to additional measures. Although we believe that the issue of interference is critical, we would question the assumption about the direction of causality between it and the broader relationship between the West and Russia. In addition, although the need for additional agreed-upon measures among states cannot be ruled out, the assumption that such agreements are necessary prevented the group from weighing possible alternatives at the national level, among the states primarily concerned, or among states and nonstate stakeholders. Second, we disagree with the suggestion that the UN is the most suitable platform for a broader discussion on this topic. The relevance of interference to actors beyond governments is clear; therefore, the involvement of civil society organizations and the private sector is a necessity. We do not believe that the UN could provide a setting for such multistakeholder engagement in the

---

[2] This text was written before the events of February 2022; in the environment that now prevails, a collaborative project like this would have been impossible. In order to share the ideas generated by our project but avoid any possible challenges for the contributors, we have decided to withhold their names.

current political climate. Third, we have reservations concerning Proposal 4 ("develop technical measures to demonstrate compliance with self-restraint commitments"). Even though the International Committee of the Red Cross recently made a similar proposal to develop a "digital watermark" to identify certain actors or infrastructure in cyberspace that must be protected (such as objects that enjoy specific protection under international humanitarian law), our group did not sufficiently consider the feasibility of the proposal and its potential negative consequences: in particular, how such tokens could become targets for malicious actors. Fourth, we cannot fully support Proposal 5. We have concerns about the current trend of origin-based online content regulation (including discriminatory regulatory measures), which could pose a threat to freedom of expression and to transnational communication. Guidelines for social media providers that require more transparency about artificial amplification are welcome but should apply universally, not just to content originating from outside a given state's borders.

Statement by the Russian Contributors[3]

It was a difficult task for experts from the United States, the EU, and Russia to find consensus. The proposals are a significant step forward, given the fundamental political contradictions between the parties regarding this issue. The issue remains contentious, which is noticeable in the discussion and the text. The Russian participants offer the following four reservations and concerns about the proposals. First, as the comparison of grievances states, the foreign financing of parties and other groups is, in fact, a shared concern among Russia, the EU, and the United States. Although the broader group did not come to a consensus about a proposal to address this problem, the Russian participants suggest that states should agree that funding certain types of activities should be considered unacceptable behavior. Second,

---

[3] This text was written before the events of February 2022; in the environment that now prevails, a collaborative project like this would have been impossible. In order to share the ideas generated by our project but avoid any possible challenges for the contributors, we have decided to withhold their names.

Proposal 4 on tokens requires careful consideration and must be evaluated further by technical experts to ensure that tokens are not used by malicious actors as "bullseyes" for attacks. Tokens could invite, rather than dissuade, cyber espionage in which a leak or other malicious use is a likely goal. Third, although the basic premise of Proposal 5 on social media is reasonable, it largely ignores the fact that most social media platforms that would be affected by any potential agreement are U.S.-based; hence, the United States has disproportionate leverage vis-à-vis these companies compared with Russia. Moreover, the social media platforms do not always comply with local regulations or requests. Alongside coordinated guidelines that encourage the social media platforms to limit cross-border artificial amplification, the three parties (Russia, the United States, and the EU) could consider discussing rules to be adopted for social media companies at the UN level. Fourth, Proposal 6 on relaxing restrictions on foreign broadcasters would require all states in question to make national decisions on media regulations. These are sovereign decisions, and state sovereignty should be respected.

Abbreviations

BBC	British Broadcasting Company
CEC	Central Elections Commission (Russia)
COVID-19	coronavirus disease 2019
DDoS	distributed denial-of-service
DW	Deutsche Welle
EU	European Union
FARA	Foreign Agents Registration Act
INCSEA	Incidents at Sea Agreement
IP	internet protocol
NGO	nongovernmental organization
PoC	point of contact
RFE/RL	Radio Free Europe/Radio Liberty
UK	United Kingdom
UN	United Nations
VOA	Voice of America

References

Agence France-Presse, "Germany Probes Claims of Pre-Election MP Hacking by Russia," *France24*, September 9, 2021. As of September 21, 2021:
https://www.france24.com/en/live-news/20210909-germany-probes-claims-of-pre-election-mp-hacking-by-russia

Appell, Mikayla, "A New Responsibility for Internet Platforms: Germany's New Hate Speech Law," American Institute for Contemporary German Studies, January 23, 2018. As of September 21, 2021:
https://www.aicgs.org/2018/01/a-new-responsibility-for-internet-platforms-germanys-new-hate-speech-law/

Arthur, Charles, "Twitter to Introduce PhotoDNA System to Block Child Abuse Images," *The Guardian*, July 22, 2013. As of September 20, 2021:
https://www.theguardian.com/technology/2013/jul/22/twitter-photodna-child-abuse

Asmolov, Gregory, "The Effects of Participatory Propaganda: From Socialization to Internalization of Conflicts," *Journal of Design and Science*, August 7, 2019.

Biden, Joseph R., Jr., and Michael Carpenter, "How to Stand Up to the Kremlin: Defending Democracy Against Its Enemies," *Foreign Affairs*, January/February 2018.

Byrne, Andrew, "Macedonia's Fake News Industry Sets Sights on Europe," *Financial Times*, December 15, 2016.

Chadwick, Lauren, "Lithuania Follows Latvia in Banning Russian Broadcaster RT," *Euronews*, July 9, 2020. As of September 20, 2021:
https://www.euronews.com/2020/07/09/lithuania-follows-latvia-in-banning-russian-broadcaster-rt

Christchurch Call, "Supporters," webpage, undated. As of September 20, 2021:
https://www.christchurchcall.com/supporters.html

Cognitive Security Collaborative, "AMITT Use Cases," webpage, March 11, 2021. As of October 14, 2021:
https://github.com/cogsec-collaborative/AMITT/blob/main/AMITT_GUIDES/03_AMITT_Use_Cases.pdf

Defending Elections Against Trolls from Enemy Regimes (DETER) Act, S. 1328, 116th Congress, 2019. As of October 14, 2021:
https://www.congress.gov/bill/116th-congress/senate-bill/1328/text

Director of National Intelligence, "DNI Coats Statement on the Intelligence Community's Response to Executive Order 13848 on Imposing Certain Sanctions in the Event of Foreign Interference in a United States Election," press release, Washington, D.C., December 21, 2018. As of September 21, 2021: https://www.dni.gov/index.php/newsroom/press-releases/press-releases-2018/ item/1933-dni-coats-statement-on-the-intelligence-community-s-response- to-executive-order-13848-on-imposing-certain-sanctions-in-the-event-of- foreign-interference-in-a-united-states-election

European Commission, Directorate-General for Communications Networks, Content and Technology, *Tackling Online Disinformation: A European Approach*, Brussels, COM(2018)236, April 26, 2018. As of September 21, 2021: https://ec.europa.eu/transparency/documents-register/ detail?ref=COM(2018)236&lang=en

European Commission, Directorate-General for Justice and Consumers, *Commission Recommendation on Election Cooperation Networks, Online Transparency, Protection Against Cybersecurity Incidents and Fighting Disinformation Campaigns in the Context of Elections to the European Parliament: A Contribution from the European Commission to the Leaders' Meeting in Salzburg on 19-20 September 2018*, Brussels, C(2018)5949, September 12, 2018a. As of September 21, 2021: https://ec.europa.eu/transparency/documents-register/ detail?ref=C(2018)5949&lang=en

———, *Securing Free and Fair European Elections: A Contribution from the European Commission to the Leaders' Meeting in Salzburg on 19-20 September 2018*, Brussels, COM(2018)637, September 12, 2018b. As of September 21, 2021: https://ec.europa.eu/transparency/documents-register/ detail?ref=COM(2018)637&lang=en

———, *Commission Guidance on the Application of Union Data Protection Law in the Electoral Context: A Contribution from the European Commission to the Leaders' Meeting in Salzburg on 19-20 September 2018*, Brussels, COM(2018)638, October 1, 2018c. As of September 21, 2021: https://ec.europa.eu/transparency/documents-register/ detail?ref=COM(2018)638&lang=EL

European Commission for Democracy Through Law, *On the Compatibility with International Human Rights Standards of a Series of Bills Introduced by the Russian State Duma Between 10 and 23 November 2020 to Amend Laws Affecting "Foreign Agents,"* Strasbourg, France, CDL-AD(2021)027, July 6, 2021. As of September 20, 2021: https://www.venice.coe.int/webforms/documents/?pdf=CDL-AD(2021)027-e

European Commission, High Representative of the Union for Foreign Affairs and Security Policy, *Tackling COVID-19 Disinformation – Getting the Facts Right*, Brussels, JOIN(2020)8, June 10, 2020. As of September 21, 2021:
https://ec.europa.eu/info/sites/default/files/
communication-tackling-covid-19-disinformation-getting-facts-right_en.pdf

European Commission, *Joint Framework on Countering Hybrid Threats: A European Union Response*, Brussels, JOIN(2016)18, April 6, 2016. As of September 21, 2021:
https://eur-lex.europa.eu/legal-content/EN/
TXT/?uri=CELEX%3A52016JC0018

———, *Report on the Implementation of the Action Plan Against Disinformation*, Brussels, JOIN(2019)12, June 14, 2019. As of October 14, 2021:
https://www.eumonitor.eu/9353000/1/j4nvhdfdk3hydzq_j9vvik7m1c3gyxp/
vkzck1ypqjth

———, "EU-Russia Relations: Commission and High Representative Propose the Way Forward," press release, Brussels, June 16, 2021. As of February 4, 2022:
https://ec.europa.eu/commission/presscorner/detail/en/ip_21_3010

European Council, "European Council Meeting (19 and 20 March 2015) – Conclusions," Brussels, EUCO 11/15, March 20, 2015. As of October 14, 2021:
https://data.consilium.europa.eu/doc/document/ST-11-2015-INIT/en/pdf

———, "Russia: Declaration by the High Representative on Behalf of the European Union on the State Duma, Regional and Local Elections," press release, Brussels, September 20, 2021. As of September 21, 2021:
https://www.consilium.europa.eu/en/press/press-releases/2021/09/20/russia-
declaration-by-the-high-representative-on-behalf-of-the-european-union-on-
the-state-duma-regional-and-local-elections/

European Parliament, Resolution of 23 November 2016 on EU Strategic Communication to Counteract Propaganda Against It by Third Parties, TA(2016)0441, November 23, 2016. As of September 21, 2021:
https://www.europarl.europa.eu/doceo/document/
TA-8-2016-0441_EN.html?redirect

———, "EU to Take Action Against Fake News and Foreign Election Interference," press release, Brussels, October 10, 2019. As of September 21, 2021:
https://www.europarl.europa.eu/news/en/press-room/20191007IPR63550/
eu-to-take-action-against-fake-news-and-foreign-electoral-interference

———, "Priority Question for Written Answer P-003967/2019: Russian Interference in European Democracies," November 21, 2019. As of September 20, 2021:
https://www.europarl.europa.eu/doceo/
document/P-9-2019-003967_EN.html#def1

European Parliament and Council of the European Union, Regulation (EU, Euratom) 2019/493 of the European Parliament and of the Council of 25 March 2019 Amending Regulation (EU, Euratom) No 1141/2014 as Regards a Verification Procedure Related to Infringements of Rules on the Protection of Personal Data in the Context of Elections to the European Parliament, March 27, 2019. As of September 21, 2021:
https://op.europa.eu/en/publication-detail/-/publication/0e1c8aa8-505e-11e9-a8ed-01aa75ed71a1/language-en

European People's Party, "Position Paper on Russia," Brussels, September 27, 2017. As of September 21, 2021:
https://www.eppgroup.eu/newsroom/publications/position-paper-on-russia

Federation Council, "Vremennaya komissiya Soveta Federatsii po zashchite gosudarstvennogo suvereniteta i predotvarashcheniyu vmeshatel'stva vo vnutrennie dela Rossiiskoi Federatsii," webpage, undated. As of September 21, 2021:
http://council.gov.ru/structure/commissions/iccf_def/

―――, *Ezhegodnyi dokald Vremennoi komissii Soveta Federatsii po zashchite gosudarstvennogo suvereniteta i predotvarshcheniyu vmeshatel'stva vo vnutrennie dela Rossiiskoi Federatsii*, Moscow, June 15, 2020a.

―――, "O massovom primenenii zakona ob inostrannykh agentakh v Rossii rechi ne idet – A. Klimov," webpage, December 9, 2020b. As of September 20, 2021:
http://council.gov.ru/events/news/122109/

"Full Transcript: FBI Director James Comey Testifies on Russian Interference in 2016 Election," *Washington Post*, March 20, 2017. As of September 21, 2021:
https://www.washingtonpost.com/news/post-politics/wp/2017/03/20/full-transcript-fbi-director-james-comey-testifies-on-russian-interference-in-2016-election/

Gatehouse, Gabriel, "Marine Le Pen: Who's Funding France's Far Right?" *BBC News*, April 3, 2017. As of September 21, 2021:
https://www.bbc.com/news/world-europe-39478066

Herb, Jeremy, Brian Fung, Jennifer Hansler, and Zachary Cohen, "Russian Hackers Targeting State and Local Governments Have Stolen Data, US Officials Say," *CNN*, October 23, 2020. As of September 21, 2021:
https://www.cnn.com/2020/10/22/politics/russian-hackers-election-data/index.html

Hoell, Maximilian, "The P5 Process: Ten Years On," London: European Leadership Network, September 2019. As of September 20, 2021:
https://www.europeanleadershipnetwork.org/wp-content/uploads/2019/09/190925-P5-Process-Max-Hoell-1.pdf

Hunt, Heather H., Chief of the FARA Registration Unit, Department of Justice, "Obligation of RTTV America, Inc., to Register Under the Foreign Agents Registration Act," letter to RTTV America, Inc., Washington, D.C., August 17, 2017. As of September 21, 2021:
https://www.justice.gov/nsd-fara/page/file/1282086/download

———, "Obligation of RIA Global LLC to Register Under the Foreign Agents Registration Act," letter to Mindia Gavasheli, Peter Martinichev, and Anastasia Sheveleva at RIA Global LLC, Washington, D.C., January 5, 2018. As of September 21, 2021:
https://www.justice.gov/nsd-fara/page/file/1282141/download

International Court of Justice, Military and Paramilitary Activities in and Against Nicaragua (Nicaragua v. United States of America), Merits, Judgment, I.C.J. Reports 1986, p. 14. As of September 20, 2021:
https://www.icj-cij.org/public/files/case-related/70/
070-19860627-JUD-01-00-EN.pdf

Kamyshev, Dmitrii, Michal Zygar', Irina Nagornykh, and Viktor Khamraev, "Vladimir Putin ostavil za soboi finansirovanie obshchestvennosti," Kommersant, November 25, 2005, p. 1. As of September 20, 2021:
https://www.kommersant.ru/doc/629603

Keitner, Chimène I., "Foreign Election Interference and International Law," in Duncan B. Hollis and Jens David Ohlin, eds., Defending Democracies: Combating Foreign Election Interference in a Digital Age, New York: Oxford University Press, 2021, pp. 179–196.

"Khakery usilenno atakuyut sait TsIK Rossii," RIA Novosti, March 4, 2012. As of September 20, 2021:
https://ria.ru/20120304/584414736.html

Klimburg, Alexander, "Of Ships and Cyber: Transposing the Incidents at Sea Agreement," Center for Strategic and International Studies, September 28, 2022.

Lange, Alethea, and Rena Coen, "How Does the Internet Know Your Race?" Center for Democracy and Technology, September 7, 2016. As of February 4, 2022:
https://cdt.org/insights/how-does-the-internet-know-your-race/

Latukhina, Kira, "Peskov nazval novye sanktsii SShA i ES vmestal'stvom v dela Rossii," Rossiiskaya Gazeta, March 3, 2021. As of September 20, 2021:
https://rg.ru/2021/03/03/peskov-nazval-novye-sankcii-ssha-i-es-
vmeshatelstvom-v-dela-rossii.html

Lynch, Sarah N., "U.S. Prosecutors Drop Mueller-Era Case Against Russian Firm," Reuters, March 16, 2020. As of September 20, 2021:
https://www.reuters.com/article/us-usa-trump-russia-concord/
u-s-prosecutors-drop-mueller-era-case-against-russian-firm-idUSKBN21405P

Meta, "Inauthentic Behavior," webpage, undated. As of February 4, 2022:
https://transparency.fb.com/policies/community-standards/
inauthentic-behavior/

———, "Preparing for Elections," webpage, 2021. As of September 20, 2021:
https://about.facebook.com/actions/preparing-for-elections-on-facebook/

Ministry of Foreign Affairs of the Russian Federation, "Comments of A.K.
Lukashevicha, Official Representative of the Ministry of Foreign Affairs
of Russia on the Termination of Activities of the United States Agency
for International Development of the Russian Federation," webpage,
September 19, 2012. As of September 20, 2021:
https://www.mid.ru/web/guest/foreign_policy/news/-/asset_publisher/
cKNonkJE02Bw/content/id/142978?p_p_id=101_INSTANCE_
cKNonkJE02Bw&_101_INSTANCE_cKNonkJE02Bw_languageId=en_GB

———, "Brifing ofitsial'nogo predstavitelya MID Rossii M.V. Zakharovoi,
Moskva, 28 dekabrya 2017 goda," webpage, December 28, 2017. As of
October 15, 2021:
http://www.mid.ru/ru/foreign_policy/news/-/asset_publisher/cKNonkJE02Bw/
content/id/3012378

———, "Comment by the Information and Press Department on the Demarche
Presented to the US Embassy," webpage, August 9, 2019. As of September 20,
2021:
https://www.mid.ru/ru/foreign_policy/news/-/asset_publisher/
cKNonkJE02Bw/content/id/3753951?p_p_id=101_INSTANCE_
cKNonkJE02Bw&_101_INSTANCE_cKNonkJE02Bw_languageId=en_GB

———, "Ob ob"yavlenii 'persona non grata" sotrudnikov diplomaticheskikh
predstavitel'stv Shvetsii, Pol'shi i Germanii," webpage, February 5, 2021. As of
February 18, 2022:
https://archive.mid.ru/ru/foreign_policy/news/-/asset_publisher/
cKNonkJE02Bw/content/id/4553276

Ministry of Justice of the Russian Federation, "Vedenie reestra inostrannykh
sredstv massovoi informatsii vypolnyayushchikh funkstii inostrannogo
agenta," webpage, June 11, 2020. As of September 20, 2021:
https://minjust.gov.ru/ru/documents/7738/

———, "Reestr inostrannykh sredstv massovoi informatsii,
vypolnyayushchikh funkstii inostrannogo agenta," webpage, September 3,
2021. As of September 20, 2021:
https://minjust.gov.ru/ru/documents/7755/

Morris, Loveday, "Germany Complains to Moscow over Pre-Election
Phishing Attacks on Politicians," Washington Post, September 6, 2021. As of
September 21, 2021:
https://www.washingtonpost.com/world/germany-russia-cyber-
attack/2021/09/06/7b9ca734-0f28-11ec-baca-86b144fc8a2d_story.html

"MVD soobshchilo o kiberatake na GAS 'Vybory,'" *Kommersant*, March 18, 2018. As of September 20, 2021:
https://www.kommersant.ru/doc/3577539

National Intelligence Council, *Foreign Threats to the 2020 US Federal Elections*, Washington, D.C., ICA 2020-00078D, March 10, 2021. As of September 21, 2021:
https://www.dni.gov/files/ODNI/documents/assessments/CA-declass-16MAR21.pdf

Nicas, Jack, "Why Can't the Social Networks Stop Fake Accounts?" *New York Times*, December 8, 2020. As of September 20, 2021:
https://www.nytimes.com/2020/12/08/technology/why-cant-the-social-networks-stop-fake-accounts.html

Office of the Special Counsel, *Report on the Investigation into Russian Interference in the 2016 Presidential Election*, Vol. 1, Washington, D.C.: U.S. Department of Justice, March 2019. As of September 21, 2021:
https://www.justice.gov/archives/sco/file/1373816/download

P5 Working Group on the Glossary of Key Nuclear Terms, *P5 Glossary of Key Nuclear Terms*, Beijing: China Atomic Energy Press, April 2015. As of September 20, 2021:
https://2009-2017.state.gov/documents/organization/243293.pdf

"Peskov: Putin ne figuriruet v publikatsii o tainykh ofshornykh schetakh," *RIA Novosti*, April 4, 2016. As of September 20, 2021:
https://ria.ru/20160404/1402162598.html

President of Russia, "Truth and Justice Regional and Local Media Forum," April 7, 2016. As of September 20, 2021:
http://en.kremlin.ru/events/president/news/51685

———,"Interv'yu avstriiskomu telekanalu ORF," June 4, 2018. As of September 21, 2021:
http://kremlin.ru/events/president/news/57675

———, "V zakonodatel'stvo vneseny izmeneniya, kasayushchiesya inostrannykh SMI, vypolnyayushchikh funkstii inostrannogo agenta," December 2, 2019. As of September 26, 2021:
http://kremlin.ru/acts/news/62205

———, "Statement by President of Russia Vladimir Putin on a Comprehensive Program of Measures for Restoring the Russia-US Cooperation in the Field of International Information Security," September 25, 2020. As of September 20, 2021:
http://en.kremlin.ru/events/president/news/64086

———, "Prezident utverdil Strategiyu natsional'noi bezopasnosti," July 2, 2021. As of September 20, 2021:
http://www.kremlin.ru/events/president/news/66098

"Pri golosovanii po konstitutsii v RF fiksirovali DDoS-ataki iz SShA, Velikobritanii, Ukrainy," *TASS*, September 7, 2020. As of September 20, 2021: https://tass.ru/politika/9391631

"Putin obvinyaet SShA v provotsirovanii protestov," *BBC Russian Service*, December 8, 2011. As of September 20, 2021: https://www.bbc.com/russian/russia/2011/12/111208_putin_opposition_protests

Putin, Vladimir, "Rossiya i menyayushchiisya mir," *Moskovskie novosti*, February 27, 2012. As of February 4, 2022: https://www.mn.ru/politics/78738

"'Radio Svoboda' oshtrafovali na 79 mln rublei za otsutstveie markirovki SMI-inoagenta," *TASS*, April 16, 2021. As of September 20, 2021: https://tass.ru/obschestvo/11171375

"Roskomnadzor schel vmeshatel'stvom v vybory blokirovku instagrama Prilepina," *Interfax*, July 23, 2021. As of February 18, 2022: https://www.interfax.ru/russia/780342

Roth, Yoel, "Because of this, API-based research can't distinguish between accounts we've already identified as bad (and hidden or removed) and real, authentic ones," Twitter post, November 2, 2018. As of September 20, 2021: https://twitter.com/yoyoel/status/1058471830531465217?s=20

———, "Information Operations on Twitter: Principles, Process, and Disclosure," *Twitter Blog*, June 13, 2019. As of September 20, 2021: https://blog.twitter.com/en_us/topics/company/2019/information-ops-on-twitter

"RSE/RS trebuet otmeny prikaza Roskomnadzora o SMI – 'inoagentakh,'" *Golos Ameriki*, June 3, 2021. As of September 20, 2021: https://www.golosameriki.com/a/rfe-rl-demand-concelation-of-roscomnadzor-order-on-media-foreign-agent/5914971.html

"RT America Stripped of Congress Credentials, While State Dept Says FARA Won't Change Its Status," *RT*, November 29, 2017. As of September 20, 2021: https://www.rt.com/usa/411361-rt-congress-credentials-withdrawal/

Sabbagh, Dan, "UK Says Russia Sought to Interfere in 2019 Election by Spreading Documents Online," *The Guardian*, July 16, 2020. As of September 21, 2021: https://www.theguardian.com/uk-news/2020/jul/16/uk-says-russia-sought-to-interfere-in-2019-election-by-leaking-documents-online

Schlosberg, Justin, "In Search of Credibility: RT and the BBC in a 'Post-Truth' World," Foreign Policy Centre, March 21, 2017.

Shesgreen, Deirdre, "'Russia Is Up to Its Old Tricks': Biden Battling COVID-19 Vaccine Disinformation Campaign," *USA Today*, March 8, 2021. As of September 21, 2021:
https://www.usatoday.com/story/news/politics/2021/03/08/white-house-use-every-tool-against-russian-vaccine-disinformation/4631972001/

Smith, Catherine, "Facebook Adopts Microsoft PhotoDNA to Remove Child Pornography," *HuffPost*, July 20, 2011. As of September 20, 2021:
https://www.huffpost.com/entry/
facebook-photodna-microsoft-child-pornography_n_864695

"SShA i Britaniya gotovyat feikii ob okruzhenii Putina, soobshchil istochnik," *RIA Novosti*, July 13, 2019. As of September 20, 2021:
https://ria.ru/20190713/1556489903.html

State Duma of the Federal Assembly of the Russian Federation, "Komissiya GD vyyavla novoye popytki povliyat' na khod izbiranel'noi kampanii v Rossii," webpage, July 15, 2021. As of September 20, 2021:
http://duma.gov.ru/news/52010/

Tadtaev, Georgii, and Anna Balashova, "Roskombandor obvinil Facebook i Google vo vmeshatel'stve v vybory v Rossii," *RBC*, September 8, 2019. As of September 17, 2021:
https://www.rbc.ru/politics/08/09/2019/5d750d0a9a7947c6aebf1103

Theohary, Catherine A., "Considering the Source: Varieties of COVID-19 Information," Washington, D.C.: Congressional Research Service, IF11552, May 19, 2020. As of February 3, 2022:
https://crsreports.congress.gov/product/pdf/IF/IF11552

Tseplyaev, Vitalii, "Kuklovodstvo k deistviyu. Nikolai Patrushev – o metodakh 'tsvetnykh revolyutsii,'" *Argumenty i fakty*, June 10, 2020. As of September 21, 2021:
https://aif.ru/society/safety/kuklovodstvo_k_deystviyu_nikolay_
patrushev_o_metodah_cvetnyh_revolyuciy

"Tsentr 'Nasiliyu.net' priznali inostrannym agentom," *Novaya gazeta*, December 29, 2020. As of September 21, 2021:
https://novayagazeta.ru/
news/2020/12/29/166830-tsentr-nasiliyu-net-priznali-inostrannym-agentom

"TsIK RF soobshchil o regulyarnykh kiberatakakh na svoi sait iz SShA i Velikobritanii," *Interfax*, June 22, 2021. As of September 20, 2021:
https://www.interfax.ru/russia/773346

Twitter, "Combating Violent Extremism," *Twitter Blog*, February 5, 2016. As of September 21, 2021:
https://blog.twitter.com/en_us/a/2016/combating-violent-extremism

———, "Civic Integrity Policy," webpage, October 2021. As of February 3, 2022:
https://help.twitter.com/en/rules-and-policies/election-integrity-policy

UN—*See* United Nations.

United Nations, Charter of the United Nations, San Francisco, June 26, 1945. As of September 20, 2021:
https://www.un.org/en/about-us/un-charter/full-text

———, Official Compendium of Voluntary National Contributions on the Subject of How International Law Applies to the Use of Information and Communications Technologies by States Submitted by Participating Governmental Experts in the Group of Governmental Experts on Advancing Responsible State Behavior in Cyberspace in the Context of International Security Established Pursuant to General Assembly Resolution 73/266, A/76/136, July 13, 2021. As of September 20, 2021:
https://front.un-arm.org/wp-content/uploads/2021/08/A-76-136-EN.pdf

United Nations General Assembly, "Developments in the Field of Information and Telecommunications in the Context of International Security, and Advancing Responsible State Behaviour in the Use of Information and Communications Technologies," October 8, 2021. As of February 4, 2022:
https://undocs.org/en/A/C.1/76/L.13

United Nations Secretary-General, *Developments in the Field of Information and Telecommunications in the Context of International Security*, A/54/213, August 10, 1999. As of September 21, 2021:
https://undocs.org/A/54/213

United States v. Internet Research Agency et al., No. 1:18-cr-32, D.D.C. February 16, 2018, Doc. 1 ("Internet Research Agency Indictment"). As of September 21, 2021:
https://www.justice.gov/file/1035477/download

United States v. Netyksho et al., No. 1: 18-cr-15, D.D.C. July 13, 2018, Doc. 1 ("Netyksho Indictment"). As of September 21, 2021:
https://www.justice.gov/file/1080281/download

U.S. Agency for Global Media, "Russia Clamps Down Further on U.S. International Media," April 4, 2014. As of September 20, 2021:
https://www.usagm.gov/2014/04/04/russia-clamps-down-further-on-u-s-international-media/

U.S. Department of Justice, "Russian National Charged with Interfering in U.S. Political System," press release, Washington, D.C., October 19, 2018. As of September 21, 2021:
https://www.justice.gov/opa/pr/russian-national-charged-interfering-us-political-system

———, "Six Russian GRU Officers Charged in Connection with Worldwide Deployment of Destructive Malware and Other Disruptive Actions in Cyberspace," press release, Washington, D.C., October 19, 2020. As of September 21, 2021:
https://www.justice.gov/opa/pr/six-russian-gru-officers-charged-connection-worldwide-deployment-destructive-malware-and

U.S. Department of State, *Department of State International Cyberspace Policy Strategy*, March 2016. As of February 3, 2022:
https://2009-2017.state.gov/documents/organization/255732.pdf

U.S. Department of State, Global Engagement Center, *Pillars of Russia's Disinformation and Propaganda Ecosystem*, Washington, D.C., August 2020. As of September 20, 2021:
https://www.state.gov/wp-content/uploads/2020/08/Pillars-of-Russia%E2%80%99s-Disinformation-and-Propaganda-Ecosystem_08-04-20.pdf

U.S. Embassy in Russia, "Secretary Pompeo's Press Availability with Russian Foreign Minister Sergey Lavrov," May 14, 2019. As of September 21, 2021:
https://ru.usembassy.gov/secretary-pompeos-press-availability-with-russian-foreign-minister-sergey-lavrov/

U.S. Senate Select Committee on Intelligence, *Russian Active Measures Campaigns and Interference in the 2016 U.S. Election*, Vol. 1: *Russian Efforts Against Election Infrastructure*, 116th Congress, 1st Session, Senate Report 116-XX, undated a. As of September 21, 2021:
https://www.intelligence.senate.gov/sites/default/files/documents/Report_Volume1.pdf

———, *Russian Active Measures Campaigns and Interference in the 2016 U.S. Election*, Vol. 2: *Russia's Use of Social Media*, 116th Congress, 1st Session, Senate Report 116-XX, undated b. As of September 21, 2021:
https://www.intelligence.senate.gov/sites/default/files/documents/Report_Volume2.pdf

"V den' vyborov otrazhena DDoS-ataka na sait TsIK s IP-adresov 15 stran," *TASS*, March 18, 2018. As of September 20, 2021:
https://tass.ru/politika/5041363

Venkina, Ekaterina, "DW otvergaet ugrozy so storony Gosdumy," *Deutsche Welle*, September 4, 2019. As of September 20, 2021:
https://www.dw.com/ru/dw-отвергает-угрозы-со-стороны-госдумы/a-50290385

Vilmer, Jean-Baptiste Jeangène, "Lessons of #MacronLeaks," *Berlin Policy Journal*, August 29, 2019. As of September 30, 2021:
https://berlinpolicyjournal.com/lessons-of-macronleaks/

Vremennaya komissiya Soveta Federatsii po zashchite gosudarstvennogo suvereniteta i pretvarashcheniyu vmeshatel'stva vo vnutrennie dela Rossiiskoi Federatsii, *Spetsial'nyi doklad po itogam presidentskikh vyborov v Rossiiskoi Federatsii (2018 g.) s tochki zreniya pokushenii na rossiiskoi electoral'nyi suverenitet*, Moscow: Sovet Federatsii, undated. As of September 20, 2021:
http://council.gov.ru/media/files/
2uQuCAAwoWu0B8tiDeDExn5x9CtBkTDV.pdf

———, *Ezhegodnyi doklad*, Moscow: Sovet Federatsii, May 30, 2019. As of September 20, 2021:
http://council.gov.ru/media/files/
LIkgU7Df0m31nfswAg80N5d4TKFhy8UG.pdf

Vylegzhanin, Aleksandr, and Kirill Kritskii, "Souchastie SShA v gosudarstvennom perevorote v Kieve 2014 goda - eto mezhdunarodnoe pravonarushenie," *Mezhdunarodnaya zhizn'*, No. 3, 2019.

Welt, Cory, Kristin Archick, Rebecca M. Nelson, and Dianne E. Rennack, *U.S. Sanctions on Russia*, Washington, D.C.: Congressional Research Service, R45415, January 17, 2020. As of February 3, 2022:
https://crsreports.congress.gov/product/pdf/R/R45415/9

Winkler, David F., *Incidents at Sea: American Confrontation and Cooperation with Russia and China, 1945–2016*, Annapolis, Md.: Naval Institute Press, 2017.

YouTube, "Our Commitments: Supporting Political Integrity," webpage, undated. As of September 20, 2021:
https://www.youtube.com/howyoutubeworks/our-commitments/
supporting-political-integrity/

Zuckerberg, Mark, "The Internet Needs New Rules. Let's Start in These Four Areas," *Washington Post*, March 30, 2019.